Delicious Chicken Dishes

Delicious Chicken Dishes

Harold Wilshaw

Sundial

Contents

This title was first published in 1978
by Sundial Publications Limited
59 Grosvenor Street, London W1

Revised edition first published 1980
Fourth impression, 1981

© 1978 Hennerwood Publications Limited

ISBN 0 906320 46 1

Printed in Hong Kong

Introduction

'I want there to be no peasant in my Kingdom so poor that he is unable to have a chicken in his pot every Sunday.'

This pious hope was expressed by Henri IV of France in the sixteenth century, and although its realization has taken a long time, the poultry industry has made it a fact today. Indeed, chicken has become easily the most economical meat to buy.

Since it is also the most popular poultry for home cooking, the majority of recipes in this book are for chicken – poussins, spring chickens, roasters and boiling chickens. The book also covers other types of poultry for popular dishes. Duckling, goose and turkey receive their fair share of attention with both familiar and more unusual ways of preparing them for family meals and those special occasions.

Oven-ready chilled and frozen birds are available all year round, as is jointed poultry, either fresh, chilled or frozen. When buying fresh poultry, choose a bird with fresh-looking skin and a plump breast with a pliable breastbone. Remove the giblets from inside the bird and keep them in the refrigerator until cooking time. Fresh poultry can be kept in the refrigerator for two days at the most.

Frozen poultry should be completely thawed before cooking. Leave it in the polythene wrapping and thaw it thoroughly in the refrigerator. You should *never* try to speed up the thawing process by immersing a frozen bird in hot water.

Note:

When following the method for casseroles in this book, use a saucepan or flameproof casserole large enough to hold the pieces of poultry comfortably. After sprinkling over the flour, use a flat wooden spatula to blend in the flour and stir the ingredients.

Stock

Stock can be made from all poultry and game bones, whether raw or cooked, and the giblets, if available, can also be used. There are basically two kinds of stock, one made just with the bones and any meat scraps attached, and the other with vegetables and herbs added.

To make approximately 900 ml (1½ pints) of plain unflavoured stock, use 750 g to 1 kg (1½ to 2 lb) bones and meat scraps, 1 × 15 ml spoon (1 tablespoon) salt and 1.2 litres (2 pints) water. Put the ingredients in a saucepan and bring to the boil, skimming off the scum from the surface. Simmer for 1½ hours, then strain into a clean container.

For a flavoured stock, add the following to the plain stock after skimming: 2 peeled and chopped onions, 2 chopped celery stalks, 2 peeled and chopped carrots, and pepper and fresh or dried herbs to taste. Proceed as above. This stock is useful for making sauces and flavouring casseroles.

To be absolutely safe, stock of any kind should be boiled for a few minutes each day, then

1. Pack the stuffing firmly over the breast from the neck end

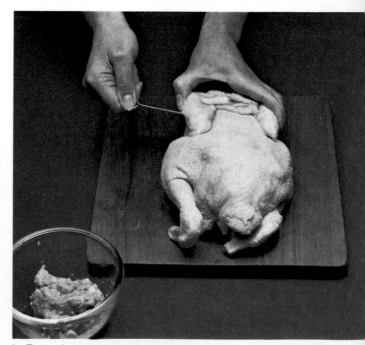

2. Press the wings against the body and pass the skewer through

cooled as quickly as possible and returned to the refrigerator for storage. Do not keep stock longer than three to four days. We all know the exaggerated stories of stockpots kept simmering for upwards of 20 years, and a fine number of churchyards they must have filled in their time.

If frozen, stock may be kept for up to 6 months. Pour the stock into a rigid container, seal, label and freeze. Alternatively, the stock may be reduced by boiling it briskly, then cooled quickly and frozen in ice cube trays. Once frozen, the cubes can be stored in a freezer bag, and can easily be added, as needed, to stews and casseroles.

Stuffing and trussing

Trussing is quite simple, and is best done using a trussing needle threaded with thin string, or skewers. First stuff the bird from the neck end: draw back the neck flap and pack the stuffing firmly over the breast. Replace the flap and reshape the breast neatly. Turn the bird over, breast downwards, and press the wings against the body. Fold the wing tips over the neck flap. Pass the needle or a skewer through the right wing, through the end of the flap and then through the left wing. If using a trussing needle, return the string over the back and knot it.

Spoon the remaining stuffing through the rear vent into the body of the bird. Turn the bird over onto its back and press the thighs against the sides of the body. Pass the needle or another skewer through the bird from one leg to the other. Tie the ends of the drumsticks neatly together with the tail stump (parson's nose).

Some recipes state that the bird should

be barded before cooking to keep the breast moist. To do this, cover the breast with thin rashers of streaky bacon, tying them on with string if necessary.

Carving

Small birds are better jointed than carved unless they are to be served whole. Chickens under 2 kg (4 lb) are best jointed after cooking. This simply entails following the method below, except that the bird is cut right through the back, which is served. Ducks cannot be carved satisfactorily, so should be divided into four.

To carve a cooked bird, place it so that the front part of the breast is towards you. Remove the trussing string or skewers, then insert the carving fork, with the guard up, into the bird towards the back. Use the fork to hold the bird securely. Slit the skin around the leg and press it gently outwards and down with the flat of the knife. Cut through the joint. Repeat with the other leg. Remove the knuckle ends of the drumsticks and divide each leg into two.

Carve the breast in slanting slices. To remove the wings, make a cut at the top of the wishbone, then turn the knife so that it presses against the carcass. Cut down and through the wing joint.

Jointing and skinning

For this operation, you will need a sharp poultry knife and shears. A poultry knife should have a long handle and a shortish blade of 15 to 18 cm (6 to 7 inches). The blade should be sharp as well as very stout so that leverage can be exerted.

To joint a bird before cooking, insert the

3. Spoon the remaining stuffing into the body of the bird

4. Pass a skewer through the bird from one leg to the other

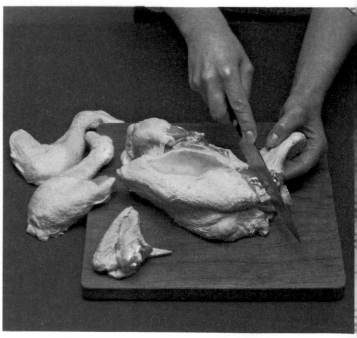

1. To remove the legs, cut through the ball and socket where the thighs meet the body of the bird

2. Remove the wings, leaving the breast intact

knife between one thigh and the body of the bird. Cut through the skin (not flesh) to the thigh joint. Push the leg away from the body until the joint is dislocated, then cut through between the ball and the socket using the point of the knife. Repeat on the other side.

If the bird is large, you may want to separate the thigh and drumstick. To do this, dislocate the joint and cut between the ball and socket in the same way.

To remove the wings, cut down to the joint where one wing joins the body, keeping as close to the joint as possible and leaving the breast intact. Insert the knife between the ball and socket and sever the wing. Cut off the wing tips, which are boney, and use them for stock. Repeat on the other side.

For a large bird, slice off part of the breast behind the wishbone; leave the breast of a smaller bird intact. Use the shears to cut along the bottom of the rib cage on each side of the breast and separate from the back by dislocating the front bones. Use the back for stock.

Divide the breast into two by cutting along one side of the breast bone with the shears. Or, the meat can be filleted off each side of the bone.

For most dishes, it is best to skin the bird, which at this stage is very simple. Just pull the skin off, cutting it where necessary.

To cut into smaller pieces, use the shears. Cut up the larger pieces so you have three pieces from each breast and two from each thigh.

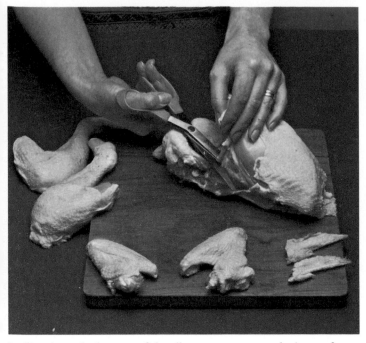

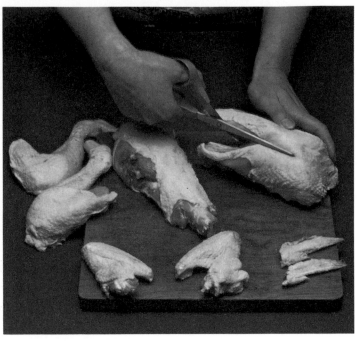

3. Cut along the bottom of the rib cage to separate the breast from the back

4. Divide the breast into two, using shears

CHICKEN

The tender white flesh of a chicken lends itself to many different methods of preparation and accompanying flavours. That, coupled with its economical price, makes it a popular choice for both family meals and entertaining.

In calculating the size of a chicken for a dish, it is usual to reckon on an average of 250 g (8 oz) per person as each portion will contain some bone. When buying chicken, or any poultry for that matter, always make sure that you get the giblets. These will make all sorts of dishes, from a good gravy, to a pâté or even part of a pie.

The chicken recipes which follow are divided into six sections: the first four contain recipes for the different kinds of chicken available – poussin, spring chicken, roasting chicken and boiler. The last two sections give recipes for chicken soups and cold chicken dishes.

From left to right: poussin, spring chicken, roasting chicken, boiler

Poussins

Poussins or baby chickens weigh between 350 and 500 g ($\frac{3}{4}$ to 1 lb). They are cooked quickly, and each will serve one to two people.

Spatchcocked poussins

Metric

4 × 350 g poussins
50 g butter, melted
Salt
Pepper
Lemon slices to garnish

Imperial

4 × 12 oz poussins
2 oz butter, melted
Salt
Pepper
Lemon slices to garnish

Cooking Time: About 20 minutes

With a sharp knife, cut through the poussins from the back, not quite severing them. Open them out and press to flatten them, fixing them open with a skewer through each. Brush with melted butter, and season with salt and pepper to taste. Cook under a preheated medium grill, turning once, until tender and brown. Brush with melted butter frequently during the cooking. Serve hot, garnished with lemon twists.

Roast poussins

Metric

4 × 350 g poussins
50 g butter, melted
Salt
Pepper
Plain flour
Watercress to garnish

Imperial

4 × 12 oz poussins
2 oz butter, melted
Salt
Pepper
Plain flour
Watercress to garnish

Cooking Time: 20–25 minutes
Oven: 200°C, 400°F, Gas Mark 6

Truss the birds. Brush with melted butter and season with salt and pepper to taste. Dredge lightly with flour and roast in a preheated moderately hot oven until tender and golden brown. Serve garnished with watercress.

Sautéed poussins

Metric

50 g butter
2 × 500 g poussins, halved
Salt
Pepper
1 × 5 ml spoon dried tarragon
75 g mushrooms, sliced
150 ml chicken stock
2 × 5 ml spoons arrowroot
1.5 × 15 ml spoons water
2 × 15 ml spoons double cream
1 × 15 ml spoon chopped fresh parsley

Imperial

2 oz butter
2 × 1 lb poussins, halved
Salt
Pepper
1 teaspoon dried tarragon
3 oz mushrooms, sliced
$\frac{1}{4}$ pint chicken stock
2 teaspoons arrowroot
1$\frac{1}{2}$ tablespoons water
2 tablespoons double cream
1 tablespoon chopped fresh parsley

Cooking Time: About 30 minutes

Melt the butter in a sauté or frying pan and brown the poussins lightly. Season with salt and pepper to taste and add the tarragon. Stir in the mushrooms and stock. Bring to the boil, cover and simmer until tender.
Transfer the poussins to a warmed serving dish. Keep hot. Dissolve the arrowroot in the water and stir into the pan. Simmer, stirring, until thickened. Stir in the cream. Taste and adjust the seasoning, and pour this sauce over the poussins. Sprinkle with the parsley and serve.

Spatchcocked poussins

Roast poussins

Sautéed poussins

Deep-fried curried poussins

Metric	Imperial
2 × 5 ml spoons curry powder	2 teaspoons curry powder
50 g plain flour	2 oz plain flour
50 g butter	2 oz butter
150 ml chicken stock	¼ pint chicken stock
1 egg	1 egg
2 × 500 g poussins, skinned and jointed	2 × 1 lb poussins, skinned and jointed
Salt	Salt
Dry breadcrumbs	Dry breadcrumbs
Oil for deep frying	Oil for deep frying
Lemon wedges to garnish	Lemon wedges to garnish

Cooking Time: About 10 minutes

Sift together the curry powder and flour. Melt the butter in a saucepan and stir in the flour and curry mixture. Cook for 1 minute, then gradually stir in the stock. Bring to the boil, stirring, and simmer until thickened and smooth. Remove from the heat and allow to cool slightly. Beat in the egg. Season the poussins with salt, then coat first with the sauce and then with the breadcrumbs. Deep fry in oil heated to 185°C, 360°F for 5 to 7 minutes or until golden brown. Drain on absorbent kitchen paper and serve hot, garnished with lemon wedges.

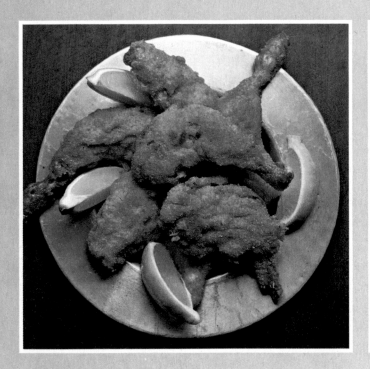

Above left: Deep-fried curried poussins
Left: Grilled spring chickens
Above: Deep-fried spring chickens
Right: Roast spring chickens

Spring chickens

Somewhat larger than poussins, these chickens weigh
750 g to 1.25 kg (1½ to 2 lb). They are usually halved to serve, and are cooked for a short time only.

Grilled spring chickens

Metric	Imperial
2 × 1 kg chickens, halved	2 × 2 lb chickens, halved
Salt	Salt
Pepper	Pepper
50 g butter, melted	2 oz butter, melted

Cooking Time: About 20 minutes

Season the birds with salt and pepper, and brush with the melted butter. Cook under a preheated hot grill until brown and tender, turning once. Brush with the melted butter frequently during cooking. Serve hot.

Deep-fried spring chickens

Metric	Imperial
Plain flour	Plain flour
Salt	Salt
Pepper	Pepper
2 × 1 kg chickens, skinned and jointed	2 × 2 lb chickens, skinned and jointed
1 egg, beaten	1 egg, beaten
150 ml milk	¼ pint milk
Dry breadcrumbs	Dry breadcrumbs
Oil for deep frying	Oil for deep frying
Parsley sprigs to garnish	Parsley sprigs to garnish

Cooking Time: About 10–15 minutes

Mix flour with salt and pepper and use to coat the chicken joints. Mix together the egg and milk. Dip the chicken joints in the egg mixture, then coat with the breadcrumbs. Deep fry in oil heated to 185°C, 360°F until golden brown, then drain on absorbent kitchen paper. Serve garnished with parsley sprigs.

Roast spring chickens

Metric	Imperial
2 × 1 kg chickens	2 × 2 lb chickens
50 g butter, melted	2 oz butter, melted
Salt	Salt
Pepper	Pepper
Watercress to garnish	Watercress to garnish

Cooking Time: 25 minutes
Oven: 200°C, 400°F, Gas Mark 6

Truss the birds and brush with melted butter. Season with salt and pepper to taste and arrange in a roasting tin. Roast in a preheated moderately hot oven until golden brown and tender. Cut in halves to serve, garnished with watercress.

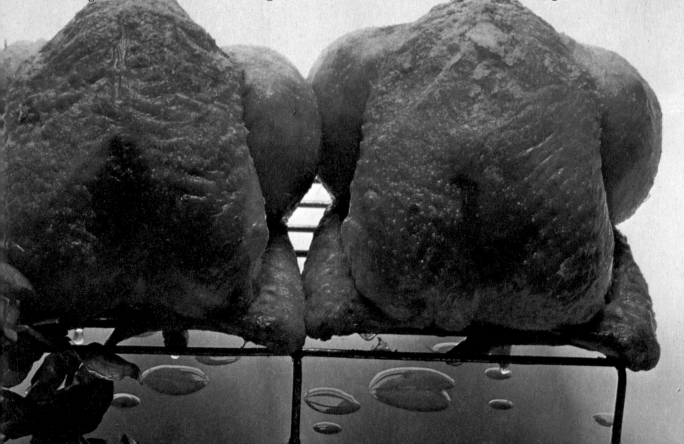

Roast stuffed spring chickens

Metric

2 × 1 kg chickens
50 g butter, melted
Fresh tarragon sprigs to
garnish

Stuffing:
25 g butter
1 onion, peeled and finely
chopped
50 g fresh breadcrumbs
1 × 5 ml spoon dried
tarragon
120 ml milk
1 egg, beaten
Salt
Pepper

Imperial

2 × 2 lb chickens
2 oz butter, melted
Fresh tarragon sprigs to
garnish

Stuffing:
1 oz butter
1 onion, peeled and finely
chopped
2 oz fresh breadcrumbs
1 teaspoon dried tarragon
4 fl oz milk
1 egg, beaten
Salt
Pepper

Cooking Time: 35–40 minutes
Oven: 190°C, 375°F, Gas Mark 5

To make the stuffing, melt the butter in a saucepan and fry the onion until soft but not brown. Stir in the breadcrumbs, tarragon and milk. Cook, stirring, for 1 to 2 minutes, then remove from the heat and allow to cool. Mix in the egg and salt and pepper to taste. Use to stuff the neck ends of the birds.

Truss the chickens, brush with the melted butter and season with salt and pepper to taste. Roast in a preheated moderately hot oven until tender and golden. Garnish with fresh tarragon sprigs before serving.

Curried spring chickens

Metric

50 g butter
2 onions, peeled and
chopped
1 garlic clove, chopped
1 × 15 ml spoon curry
powder
2 × 750 g chickens,
skinned and
jointed
150ml
chicken
stock

1 × 15 ml
spoon tomato
purée
1 × 15 ml spoon
brown sugar
1 bay leaf
Salt
Pepper
Lemon slices
to garnish

Imperial

2 oz butter
2 onions, peeled and
chopped
1 garlic clove, chopped
1 tablespoon curry powder
2 × 1½ lb chickens, skinned
and jointed
¼ pint chicken stock
1 tablespoon tomato purée
1 tablespoon brown sugar
1 bay leaf
Salt
Pepper
Lemon slices to garnish

Cooking Time: About 50 minutes

Melt the butter in a frying pan and fry the onions, garlic and curry powder for 2 minutes. Add the chicken pieces and continue to fry for 5 to 6 minutes. Moisten with the stock and add the tomato purée, sugar, bay leaf and salt and pepper to taste. Cover and simmer gently for 40 minutes or until the chicken is cooked.

Remove the bay leaf. Adjust the seasoning and serve on a bed of plain boiled rice, garnished with lemon slices.

Below left: Curried spring chickens
Right: Roast stuffed chicken
Below right: Roast stuffed spring chickens

Roasters

The vast majority of chickens sold are roasters, which start in weight at 1.5 kg (3 lb).

Roast stuffed chicken

Metric	Imperial
1 × 1.75 kg chicken	1 × 3½ lb chicken
50 g butter, melted	2 oz butter, melted
Watercress to garnish	Watercress to garnish
Stuffing:	Stuffing:
25 g butter	1 oz butter
1 onion, peeled and chopped	1 onion, peeled and chopped
100 g pork sausagemeat	4 oz pork sausagemeat
75 g fresh breadcrumbs	3 oz fresh breadcrumbs
1 × 5 ml spoon dried mixed herbs	1 teaspoon dried mixed herbs
1 egg, beaten	1 egg, beaten
Salt	Salt
Pepper	Pepper

Cooking Time: About 1 hour
Oven: 180°C, 350°F, Gas Mark 4

To make the stuffing, melt the butter in a frying pan and fry the onion until it is soft but not brown. Mix in the sausagemeat, breadcrumbs and herbs. Remove from the heat and allow to cool, then stir in the egg and salt and pepper to taste. Use to stuff the chicken.

Truss the bird, brush with the melted butter and season with salt and pepper to taste. Roast in a preheated moderate oven, basting once or twice, until tender and golden. Serve garnished with watercress.

Tarragon chicken

Metric	Imperial
50 g butter	2 oz butter
1 × 1.75 kg chicken, skinned and jointed	1 × 3½ lb chicken, skinned and jointed
2 onions, peeled and chopped	2 onions, peeled and chopped
40 g plain flour	1½ oz plain flour
2 × 15 ml spoons chopped fresh tarragon	2 tablespoons chopped fresh tarragon
450 ml chicken stock	¾ pint chicken stock
Salt	Salt
Pepper	Pepper

Cooking Time: About 1¼ hours

Melt the butter in a flameproof casserole. Add the chicken and onions and fry until the chicken joints are browned. Sprinkle over the flour and stir well. Continue to cook, allowing the flour mixture to colour lightly. Stir in 1 × 15 ml spoon (1 tablespoon) of the tarragon and the stock. Bring to the boil and skim. Add salt and pepper to taste and cover. Simmer gently for 1 hour or until tender. Just before serving, adjust the seasoning and sprinkle over the remaining tarragon.

Coq au vin

Metric	Imperial
50 g butter	2 oz butter
175 g piece collar of bacon, diced	6 oz piece collar of bacon, diced
2 onions, peeled and chopped	2 onions, peeled and chopped
2 garlic cloves, chopped	2 garlic cloves, chopped
1 × 2 kg chicken, skinned and jointed	1 × 4 lb chicken, skinned and jointed
50 g plain flour	2 oz plain flour
150 ml chicken stock	¼ pint chicken stock
300 ml dry red wine	½ pint dry red wine
Salt	Salt
Pepper	Pepper
6–8 mushrooms, sliced	6–8 mushrooms, sliced
1 × 15 ml spoon tomato purée	1 tablespoon tomato purée
1 bay leaf	1 bay leaf
Fried bread triangles to garnish	Fried bread triangles to garnish

Cooking Time: About 1¼ hours

Melt the butter in a flameproof casserole and fry the bacon, onions, garlic and chicken pieces until evenly browned. Sprinkle over the flour and stir well. Cook until lightly coloured, then stir in the stock and wine. Season with salt and pepper to taste. Add the mushrooms, tomato purée and bay leaf. Cover and simmer gently for 1 hour.
Remove the bay leaf and adjust the seasoning. Serve garnished with fried bread triangles.

Left: Tarragon chicken
Right: Coq au vin
Far right: Chicken casserole with mushrooms

Chicken casserole with mushrooms

Metric	Imperial
0 g butter	2 oz butter
× 2 kg chicken, skinned and jointed	1 × 4 lb chicken, skinned and jointed
onion, peeled and chopped	1 onion, peeled and chopped
0 g plain flour	¾ oz plain flour
00 ml chicken stock	½ pint chicken stock
25 g mushrooms, sliced	8 oz mushrooms, sliced
× 15 ml spoon soy sauce	1 tablespoon soy sauce
2 × 5 ml spoons Worcestershire sauce	2 teaspoons Worcestershire sauce
Salt	Salt
Pepper	Pepper

Cooking Time: About 1¼ hours

Melt the butter in a flameproof casserole. Add the chicken and onion and fry until the chicken joints are browned. Sprinkle over the flour and cook, stirring, for 1 minute. Stir in the stock. Bring to the boil and skim. Stir in the mushrooms and soy and Worcestershire sauces with salt and pepper to taste. Cover and simmer gently for 1 hour or until the chicken is tender. Adjust the seasoning before serving.

CHICKEN

Chicken casserole with tomato and celery

Metric	Imperial
50 g butter	2 oz butter
1 × 1.75 kg chicken, quartered or 4 chicken portions	1 × 3½ lb chicken, quartered or 4 chicken portions
2 onions, peeled and chopped	2 onions, peeled and chopped
2 garlic cloves, crushed	2 garlic cloves, crushed
1 head of celery, cut into 2.5 cm pieces	1 head of celery, cut into 1 inch pieces
1 × 15 ml spoon dried basil	1 tablespoon dried basil
1 × 400 g can tomatoes	1 × 14 oz can tomatoes
Salt	Salt
Pepper	Pepper

Cooking Time: About 1¾ hours
Oven: 180°C, 350°F, Gas Mark 4

Melt the butter in a flameproof casserole and fry the chicken, onions and garlic until the chicken is browned. Add the celery, basil and tomatoes with the can juice and season with salt and pepper to taste. Cover and transfer to a preheated moderate oven. Cook for 1½ hours. Adjust the seasoning before serving.

Chicken provençale

Metric	Imperial
120 ml olive oil	4 fl oz olive oil
1 × 1.75 kg chicken, quartered or 4 chicken portions	1 × 3½ lb chicken, quartered or 4 chicken portions
2 onions, peeled and chopped	2 onions, peeled and chopped
2 garlic cloves, crushed	2 garlic cloves, crushed
2 green peppers, cored, seeded and finely diced	2 green peppers, cored, seeded and finely diced
150 ml dry white wine	¼ pint dry white wine
6 tomatoes, skinned and chopped	6 tomatoes, skinned and chopped
1 × 15 ml spoon tomato purée	1 tablespoon tomato purée
1 bay leaf	1 bay leaf
1 × 5 ml spoon dried oregano	1 teaspoon dried oregano
Salt	Salt
Pepper	Pepper

Cooking Time: About 1½ hours

Heat the oil in a flameproof casserole and fry the chicken, onions, garlic and green peppers until the chicken is browned. Add the wine, tomatoes, tomato purée, bay leaf and oregano. Season with salt and pepper to taste. Cover and simmer for 1¼ hours.
Remove the bay leaf and adjust the seasoning. Serve with saffron rice.

Madras curry

Metric	Imperial
50 g butter or dripping	2 oz butter or dripping
1 × 1.5 kg chicken, jointed	1 × 3 lb chicken, jointed
2 onions, peeled and chopped	2 onions, peeled and chopped
50 g hot curry powder	2 oz hot curry powder
2 garlic cloves, chopped	2 garlic cloves, chopped
900 ml chicken stock	1½ pints chicken stock
Juice of ½ lemon	Juice of ½ lemon
2 × 15 ml spoons tomato purée	2 tablespoons tomato purée
1 × 15 ml spoon demerara sugar	1 tablespoon demerara sugar
2 bay leaves	2 bay leaves
Salt	Salt
Pepper	Pepper

Cooking Time: About 1¾ hours

Melt the butter or dripping in a flameproof casserole and fry the chicken pieces, onions and curry powder together until the chicken is evenly browned. Add the garlic, then stir in the stock, lemon juice, tomato purée, sugar and bay leaves. Season with salt and pepper to taste. Cover and simmer for 1½ hours.
Remove the bay leaves and adjust the seasoning. Serve with plain boiled rice, poppadoms, coconut, chutney and hot pickles.

Madras curry; Chicken casserole with tomato and celery; Chicken provençale

18

Chasseur chicken

Metric	Imperial
50 g butter	2 oz butter
1 × 1.75 kg chicken, jointed	1 × 3½ lb chicken, jointed
6 streaky bacon rashers, rinds removed, cut into 4 pieces	6 streaky bacon rashers, rinds removed, cut into 4 pieces
2 onions, peeled and finely chopped	2 onions, peeled and finely chopped
50 g plain flour	2 oz plain flour
150 ml dry red wine	¼ pint dry red wine
600 ml chicken stock	1 pint chicken stock
3 tomatoes, skinned and chopped	3 tomatoes, skinned and chopped
250 g mushrooms, sliced	8 oz mushrooms, sliced
2 bay leaves	2 bay leaves
1 × 15 ml spoon soy sauce	1 tablespoon soy sauce
Salt	Salt
Pepper	Pepper

Cooking Time: About 1¼ hours

Melt the butter in a flameproof casserole and fry the chicken pieces with the bacon and onions until the chicken is browned. Sprinkle the flour into the casserole and cook, stirring, for 1 minute. Stir in the wine and stock. Bring to the boil and skim. Add the tomatoes, mushrooms, bay leaves, soy sauce and salt and pepper to taste. Cover and simmer gently for 1 hour. Remove the bay leaves and adjust the seasoning before serving.

Chicken with olives

Metric	Imperial
50 g butter	2 oz butter
1 × 1.5 kg chicken, skinned and cut into small pieces	1 × 3 lb chicken, skinned and cut into small pieces
1 onion, peeled and chopped	1 onion, peeled and chopped
1 garlic clove, crushed	1 garlic clove, crushed
600 ml chicken stock	1 pint chicken stock
1 fresh thyme sprig	1 fresh thyme sprig
Salt	Salt
Pepper	Pepper
2 × 5 ml spoons arrowroot	2 teaspoons arrowroot
1.5 × 15 ml spoons water	1½ tablespoons water
1 × 150 g jar stuffed green olives, drained	1 × 5 oz jar stuffed green olives, drained

Cooking Time: About 1½ hours

Melt the butter in a saucepan and fry the chicken pieces, onion and garlic until the chicken is lightly browned. Stir in the stock and bring to the boil. Skim. Add the sprig of thyme and salt and pepper to taste. Cover and simmer for 1 hour.

Transfer the chicken pieces to a warmed serving dish and keep hot. Dissolve the arrowroot in the water and add to the saucepan. Simmer, stirring, until thickened. Stir in the olives and heat through. Taste and adjust the seasoning. Pour this sauce over the chicken pieces and serve.

Below left: Chasseur chicken
Below: Chicken with olives
Right: Chicken Maryland

Chicken Maryland

Metric	Imperial
1 × 1.5 kg chicken, skinned and quartered, or 4 chicken portions	*1 × 3 lb chicken, skinned and quartered, or 4 chicken portions*
25 g plain flour	*1 oz plain flour*
Salt	*Salt*
Pepper	*Pepper*
2 eggs	*2 eggs*
150 ml milk	*¼ pint milk*
175–225 g dry breadcrumbs	*6–8 oz dry breadcrumbs*
2 bananas, peeled and halved	*2 bananas, peeled and halved*
4 streaky bacon rashers, rinds removed	*4 streaky bacon rashers, rinds removed*
Oil for deep frying	*Oil for deep frying*
1 × 225 g can sweetcorn	*1 × 8 oz can sweetcorn*
Parsley sprigs to garnish	*Parsley sprigs to garnish*

Cooking Time: About 25 minutes

Dry the chicken pieces well. Mix the flour with salt and pepper and dust over the chicken. Beat the eggs and milk together and use to coat the chicken pieces, then coat them evenly with breadcrumbs. Do the same with the halved bananas.

Put the bacon on a board and flatten well with the back of a knife. Cut each rasher into two. Roll up and secure with half wooden cocktail sticks.

Deep fry the bacon rolls in oil at 185°C, 360°F for 3 minutes or until crisp. Drain and keep hot. Fry the chicken in the oil for 12 to 15 minutes. Drain the chicken on absorbent kitchen paper and keep hot while you fry the breaded bananas for 3 to 4 minutes.

Meanwhile, heat the sweetcorn. Drain and serve with the bacon, chicken and bananas. Accompany with chips. Garnish with parsley sprigs.

Chicken casseroled with lemon and chives

Metric

50 g butter
1 × 1.5 kg chicken,
quartered or 4 chicken
portions
150 ml dry white wine
450 ml water
Thinly pared rind and
juice of 1 lemon
Salt
Pepper
3 × 15 ml spoons chopped
fresh chives or the green of
spring onions
2 × 5 ml spoons arrowroot
1 × 15 ml spoon water

Imperial

2 oz butter
1 × 3 lb chicken, quartered
or 4 chicken portions
¼ pint dry white wine
¾ pint water
Thinly pared rind and
juice of 1 lemon
Salt
Pepper
3 tablespoons chopped
fresh chives or the green
of spring onions
2 teaspoons arrowroot
1 tablespoon water

Cooking Time: About 1 hour 20 minutes

Melt the butter in a saucepan. Add the chicken quarter
and brown on all sides. Pour over the wine and the water
Add the shredded lemon rind and juice. Bring to the boi
and skim. Season with salt and pepper to taste. Cover and
simmer for 1 hour.

Ten minutes before the chicken is ready, add 2 × 15 m
spoons (2 tablespoons) of the chives or spring onions.
Transfer the chicken pieces to a warmed dish and keep hot
Dissolve the arrowroot in the water and add to the sauce in
the saucepan. Bring to the boil, stirring until thickened
Adjust the seasoning. Pour the sauce over the chicken
pieces. Sprinkle over the remaining chives or spring
onions.

Roast chicken with green butter sauce

Metric

1 × 1.75 kg chicken
Salt
Pepper
50 g butter, melted
1 × 15 ml spoon plain
flour

Sauce:
50 g butter
1 bunch of watercress,
finely chopped
1 × 15 ml spoon chopped
fresh tarragon
1 × 15 ml spoon chopped
fresh parsley
2 × 15 ml spoons chopped
raw spinach
1 × 15 ml spoon chopped
raw sorrel

Imperial

1 × 3½ lb chicken
Salt
Pepper
2 oz butter, melted
1 tablespoon plain flour

Sauce:
2 oz butter
1 bunch of watercress,
finely chopped
1 tablespoon chopped
fresh tarragon
1 tablespoon chopped
fresh parsley
2 tablespoons chopped raw
spinach
1 tablespoon chopped raw
sorrel

Cooking Time: About 1 hour 20 minutes
Oven: 200°C, 400°F, Gas Mark 6

Season the chicken with salt and pepper. Brush with the
melted butter and sprinkle with the flour. Put in a roasting
tin and roast in a preheated moderately hot oven for about
1¼ hours. Remove from the oven and keep hot on a warmed
dish.

To make the sauce, add the butter to the tin. Stir in the
remaining sauce ingredients and heat gently, stirring. If
too dry, add a little stock. Season to taste with salt and
pepper. Carve the bird. Pour over the sauce and serve.

Casserole of chicken in beer

Metric

50 g butter
1 × 1.5 kg chicken,
quartered or 4 chicken
portions
2 onions, peeled and
chopped
2 garlic cloves, crushed
900 ml light beer
50 g plain flour
175 g mushrooms, sliced
2 × 15 ml spoons tomato
purée
1 bay leaf
Salt
Pepper
Chopped parsley to garnish

Imperial

2 oz butter
1 × 3 lb chicken, quartered
or 4 chicken portions
2 onions, peeled and
chopped
2 garlic cloves, crushed
1½ pints light beer
2 oz plain flour
6 oz mushrooms, sliced
2 tablespoons tomato
purée
1 bay leaf
Salt
Pepper
Chopped parsley to garnish

Cooking Time: About 1½ hours

Melt the butter in a flameproof casserole. Add the chicken
quarters, onions and garlic and fry until the chicken pieces
are browned all over. Meanwhile, boil the beer until
reduced to 600 ml (1 pint).

Sprinkle the flour over the chicken pieces and cook,
stirring, for 1 minute. Stir in the hot beer. Bring to the boil
and skim. Cover and simmer for 10 minutes, then stir in the
mushrooms, tomato purée, bay leaf and salt and pepper to
taste. Simmer for about 1 hour or until the chicken is
tender. Remove the bay leaf and adjust the seasoning
before serving, garnished with parsley.

Chicken casseroled with lemon and chives

Roast chicken with green butter sauce

Casserole of chicken in beer

Chicken in cider with apples

Metric

1 × 1.5 kg chicken,
quartered or 4 chicken
portions
3 large cooking apples,
peeled, cored and finely
chopped
600 ml dry cider,
preferably draught
(Bulmer's No. 7)
2 bay leaves
Salt
Pepper
50 g butter
Lemon slices to garnish

Imperial

1 × 3 lb chicken, quartered
or 4 chicken portions
3 large cooking apples,
peeled, cored and finely
chopped
1 pint dry cider,
preferably draught
(Bulmer's No. 7)
2 bay leaves
Salt
Pepper
2 oz butter
Lemon slices to garnish

Cooking Time: About 1 hour

Put the chicken quarters into a saucepan that will just hold them comfortably. Pack the apples round the chicken to fill the pan almost completely. Pour over the cider to cover. Add the bay leaves and salt and pepper to taste and top with the butter. Cover and bring to the boil. Simmer gently for about 1 hour or until cooked.

Transfer the chicken to a warmed serving dish and keep hot. Remove the bay leaves. Sieve the apples and cooking juice, or liquidize. Adjust the seasoning and pour over the chicken. Garnish with lemon slices.

Chicken in white wine

Metric

50 g butter
1 × 1.5 kg chicken,
quartered or 4 chicken
portions
Salt
Pepper
25 g plain flour
300 ml dry white wine
300 ml chicken stock
(made with garlic)
2 bay leaves
1 fresh thyme sprig
Watercress to garnish

Imperial

2 oz butter
1 × 3 lb chicken, quartered
or 4 chicken portions
Salt
Pepper
1 oz plain flour
½ pint dry white wine
½ pint chicken stock (made
with garlic)
2 bay leaves
1 fresh thyme sprig
Watercress to garnish

Cooking Time: About 1¼ hours

Melt the butter in a flameproof casserole. Season the chicken pieces with salt and pepper and fry until lightly browned on all sides. Sprinkle the flour into the casserole and cook, stirring, for 2 minutes. Pour over the wine and stock and stir well. Bring to the boil and skim. Add salt and pepper to taste, the bay leaves and thyme. Cover and simmer gently for 1 hour. Remove the bay leaves and adjust the seasoning before serving, garnished with watercress.

Chicken mornay

Metric

75 g butter
1 × 1.75 kg chicken,
jointed
40 g plain flour
300 ml dry white wine
300 ml chicken stock
(made with garlic)
1 fresh thyme sprig
Salt
Pepper
100 g cheese, grated
2 egg yolks
2 × 15 ml spoons double
cream

Imperial

3 oz butter
1 × 3½ lb chicken, jointed
1½ oz plain flour
½ pint dry white wine
½ pint chicken stock (made
with garlic)
1 fresh thyme sprig
Salt
Pepper
4 oz cheese, grated
2 egg yolks
2 tablespoons double
cream

Cooking Time: About 1½ hours

Melt 50 g (2 oz) of the butter in a saucepan. Add the chicken pieces and fry lightly until golden. Sprinkle 25 g (1 oz) of the flour into the pan and cook, stirring, for 1 minute. Stir in the wine and stock. Bring to the boil and skim. Add the thyme and salt and pepper to taste. Simmer for 1 hour or until cooked. Transfer the chicken to a flameproof serving dish and keep hot.

Remove the thyme. Mix the remaining butter and flour together to make a paste. Add this in small pieces to the sauce, stirring, and cook until thickened. Stir in 75 g (3 oz) of the cheese. Remove from the heat.

Beat together the egg yolks and cream and beat into the sauce. Taste and adjust the seasoning. Pour over the chicken. Sprinkle with the remaining grated cheese and brown quickly under a preheated hot grill.

Chicken in cider with apples; Chicken in white wine; Chicken mornay

Casserole of chicken with Jerusalem artichokes

Metric	Imperial
150 g butter	5 oz butter
1 × 1.5 kg chicken, skinned and jointed	1 × 3 lb chicken, skinned and jointed
900 ml chicken stock	1½ pints chicken stock
Salt	Salt
Pepper	Pepper
500 g Jerusalem artichokes, peeled (to keep white, put them into water with a little lemon juice)	1 lb Jerusalem artichokes, peeled (to keep white, put them into water with a little lemon juice)
25 g plain flour	1 oz plain flour
2 × 15 ml spoons double cream	2 tablespoons double cream
Orange slices to garnish	Orange slices to garnish

Cooking Time: About 1 hour 20 minutes

Melt 75 g (3 oz) of the butter in a saucepan. Add the chicken pieces and fry until lightly browned on all sides. Pour in the stock and add salt and pepper to taste. Bring to the boil and cover. Simmer for 30 minutes.

Add the artichokes and bring back to the boil. Cook for a further 30 minutes. Remove the artichokes from the pan with a slotted spoon. Arrange with the chicken pieces on a warmed serving dish and keep hot.

Mix the remaining butter with the flour to make a paste. Add this, in small pieces, to the sauce and cook, stirring, until thickened. Stir in the cream. Adjust the seasoning. Pour the sauce over the chicken and artichokes and serve, garnished with orange slices.

Jugged chicken

Metric	Imperial
1 × 1.5 kg chicken, skinned and quartered, or 4 chicken portions	1 × 3 lb chicken, skinned and quartered, or 4 chicken portions
150 ml dry red wine	¼ pint dry red wine
2 onions, peeled and chopped	2 onions, peeled and chopped
2 garlic cloves, crushed	2 garlic cloves, crushed
2 bay leaves	2 bay leaves
50 g dripping	2 oz dripping
50 g plain flour	2 oz plain flour
600 ml chicken stock	1 pint chicken stock
1 × 15 ml spoon tomato purée	1 tablespoon tomato purée
Salt	Salt
Pepper	Pepper
1 × 15 ml spoon dried tarragon	1 tablespoon dried tarragon
4 × 15 ml spoons port wine	4 tablespoons port wine

Cooking Time: About 1¼ hours

Put the chicken pieces into a bowl and pour over the red wine. Add the onions, garlic and bay leaves. Leave to marinate overnight.

Remove the chicken from the marinade and pat dry with absorbent kitchen paper. Melt the dripping in a flameproof casserole. Add the chicken pieces and fry until lightly browned on all sides. Sprinkle the flour into the casserole and cook, stirring, until light brown. Stir in the marinade, stock, tomato purée, salt and pepper to taste and the tarragon. Cover and simmer for 1 hour.

Stir in the port. Remove the bay leaves and adjust the seasoning. Serve from the casserole.

Chicken Argenteuil

Metric	Imperial
75 g butter	3 oz butter
1 × 1.5 kg chicken, skinned and quartered or 4 chicken portions	1 × 3 lb chicken, skinned and quartered or 4 chicken portions
50 g plain flour	2 oz plain flour
600 ml chicken stock*	1 pint chicken stock*
Salt	Salt
Pepper	Pepper
150 ml water	¼ pint water
500 g fresh asparagus tips	1 lb fresh asparagus tips
2 × 15 ml spoons double cream	2 tablespoons double cream

Cooking Time: About 1 hour 25 minutes

Melt 25 g (1 oz) of the butter in a saucepan. Add the chicken pieces and fry until lightly browned on all sides. Sprinkle 25 g (1 oz) of the flour into the pan and cook, stirring, for 1 minute. Stir in the stock. Bring to the boil and skim. Add salt and pepper to taste. Cover and simmer for 1 hour. Transfer the chicken pieces to a warmed serving dish and keep hot.

Bring the water to the boil in a saucepan and add a pinch of salt. Add the asparagus tips and poach until just tender. Strain the cooking water into the sauce. Keep the asparagus tips hot. Mix the remaining butter and flour together to make a paste. Add this in small pieces to the sauce and cook, stirring, until thickened. Stir in the cream. Taste and adjust the seasoning.

Pour the sauce over the chicken and garnish the dish with the asparagus tips.

*Note: Use the asparagus stalks in making the stock.

Far left: Jugged chicken
Left: Chicken Argenteuil
Below: Casserole of chicken with Jerusalem artichokes

Chicken Marengo

Metric	Imperial
100 g butter	4 oz butter
1 × 1.75 kg chicken, quartered or 4 chicken portions	1 × 3½ lb chicken, quartered or 4 chicken portions
6 shallots, peeled	6 shallots, peeled
2 garlic cloves, crushed	2 garlic cloves, crushed
100 g plain flour	4 oz plain flour
6 tomatoes, skinned and quartered	6 tomatoes, skinned and quartered
175 g button mushrooms	6 oz button mushrooms
1 bay leaf	1 bay leaf
1 × 5 ml spoon dried oregano	1 teaspoon dried oregano
1 white truffle, chopped, but kept in its juice	1 white truffle, chopped, but kept in its juice
1 bottle of Marsala	1 bottle of Marsala
100 ml brandy	3 fl oz brandy

Top left: Chicken Marengo
Top right: Chicken in plum sauce
Right: Roast chicken with braised celeriac

Cooking Time: About 1½ hours

There are countless recipes for this dish, which takes its name from the battle in which Napoleon Bonaparte defeated the Austrians in 1800. Napoleon's chef, Dunand, created it on the battlefield, and it is certainly worthy of a victory feast.

Melt 75 g (3 oz) of the butter in a flameproof casserole. Add the chicken pieces, shallots and garlic and fry until the chicken is lightly browned on all sides. Sprinkle over 50 g (2 oz) of the flour and cook, stirring, for 1 minute. Add the tomatoes, mushrooms, bay leaf, oregano, truffle with its juice and Marsala. Bring to the boil and skim. Cover and simmer for 1¼ hours or until tender.

Ten minutes before the chicken is ready, add the brandy and stir well. Mix together the remaining butter and flour to make a paste. Add in small pieces to the sauce, stirring, and simmer until thickened. Remove the bay leaf and adjust the seasoning before serving.

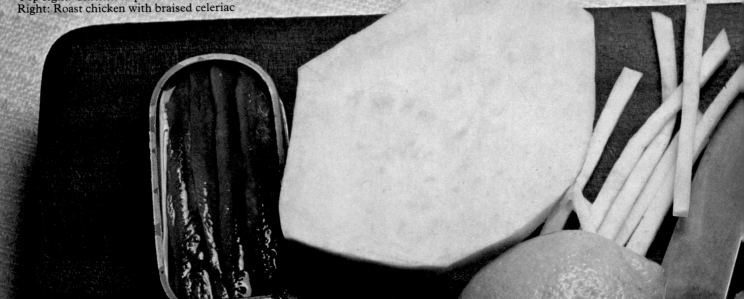

Chicken in plum sauce

Metric	Imperial
50 g butter	2 oz butter
1 × 1.5 kg chicken, jointed	1 × 3 lb chicken, jointed
1 onion, peeled and chopped	1 onion, peeled and chopped
500 g fresh plums, stoned, cooked and sieved to purée	1 lb fresh plums, stoned, cooked and sieved to purée
Juice of ½ lemon	Juice of ½ lemon
1 bay leaf	1 bay leaf
Salt	Salt
Pepper	Pepper

Cooking Time: About 1¾ hours
Oven: 180°C, 350°F, Gas Mark 4

Melt the butter in a flameproof casserole. Add the chicken and onion and fry gently until the chicken is lightly browned on all sides. Add the plum purée, lemon juice, bay leaf and salt and pepper to taste. Cover and transfer to a preheated moderate oven. Cook for 1½ hours or until tender. Remove the bay leaf and adjust the seasoning before serving.

Roast chicken with braised celeriac

Metric	Imperial
1 × 1.5 kg chicken	1 × 3 lb chicken
Salt	Salt
Pepper	Pepper
50 g butter, melted	2 oz butter, melted
1 large celeriac bulb, peeled and cut into matchsticks	1 large celeriac bulb, peeled and cut into matchsticks
Juice of ½ lemon	Juice of ½ lemon
40 g butter	1½ oz butter
1 × 50 g can anchovy fillets	1 × 2 oz can anchovy fillets
Parsley sprigs to garnish	Parsley sprigs to garnish

Cooking Time: About 1½ hours
Oven: 200°C, 400°F, Gas Mark 6

Truss the chicken and season with salt and pepper. Brush with the melted butter and place in a roasting tin. Roast in a preheated moderately hot oven for 1¼ hours, basting once or twice with the melted butter.

Meanwhile, blanch the celeriac for 4 minutes in boiling salted water with the lemon juice. Drain well.

Remove the chicken from the oven and keep hot on a warmed dish. Add the celeriac to the roasting tin with the butter. Mix well with the pan juices. Add the anchovies with their oil. Cover with foil and cook gently on top of the stove until the celeriac has softened.

Carve the chicken and arrange on a warmed serving dish. Surround with the celeriac mixture. Garnish with parsley.

Chicken with yogurt

Metric	Imperial
50 g butter	2 oz butter
1 × 1.5 kg chicken, jointed	1 × 3 lb chicken, jointed
1 onion, peeled and chopped	1 onion, peeled and chopped
½ green pepper, cored, seeded and chopped	½ green pepper, cored, seeded and chopped
1 garlic clove, crushed	1 garlic clove, crushed
65 g plain flour	2½ oz plain flour
600 ml chicken stock	1 pint chicken stock
Salt	Salt
Pepper	Pepper
2 × 150 ml cartons plain unsweetened yogurt	2 × 5 fl oz cartons plain unsweetened yogurt
Chopped fresh chervil or parsley to garnish	Chopped fresh chervil or parsley to garnish

Cooking Time: About 1¼ hours

Melt the butter in a flameproof casserole. Add the chicken pieces, onion, green pepper and garlic and fry until the chicken is lightly browned on all sides. Sprinkle over the flour and cook, stirring, for 1 minute. Stir in the stock with salt and pepper to taste. Bring to the boil and simmer for 30 minutes.

Stir in the yogurt and continue cooking very gently, covered, for 30 minutes. Adjust the seasoning. Serve garnished with chervil or parsley.

Chicken with rice

Metric	Imperial
50 g butter	2 oz butter
1 × 1.5 kg chicken, quartered or 4 chicken portions	1 × 3 lb chicken, quartered or 4 chicken portions
100 g mushrooms, sliced	4 oz mushrooms, sliced
1 onion, peeled and chopped	1 onion, peeled and chopped
300 ml water	½ pint water
Salt	Salt
Pepper	Pepper
100 g long-grain rice	4 oz long-grain rice
2 × 15 ml spoons oil	2 tablespoons oil
Pinch of saffron powder	Pinch of saffron powder

Cooking Time: About 1¼ hours

Melt the butter in a saucepan. Add the chicken pieces and fry until lightly browned on all sides. Add the mushrooms, onion, water and salt and pepper to taste. Cover and simmer for 1 hour.

Meanwhile, cook the rice in plenty of boiling salted water for 10 minutes. Drain well and fry gently in the oil with the saffron for 6 to 7 minutes.

Pile the rice on a warmed serving dish and arrange the chicken pieces and vegetables on top.

Inset left: Chicken with yogurt
Centre: Chicken Alexis Soyer
Inset right: Chicken with rice

Chicken Alexis Soyer

Metric	Imperial
2 small or 1 medium black truffle, thinly sliced	2 small or 1 medium black truffle, thinly sliced
120 ml Madeira	4 fl oz Madeira
1 × 1.75 kg chicken	1 × 3½ lb chicken
175 g liver pâté	6 oz liver pâté
100 g fresh white breadcrumbs	4 oz fresh white breadcrumbs
Salt	Salt
Pepper	Pepper
100 g butter	4 oz butter

Cooking Time: About 1½ hours
Oven: 200°C, 400°F, Gas Mark 6
     180°C, 350°F, Gas Mark 4

Alexis Soyer was chef at the Reform Club when Queen Victoria came to the throne. This dish is just one of many that he created.

Marinate the truffle in the Madeira for 1 hour. Lift the skin on the breast of the chicken by inserting your fingers from the neck end and gently easing the skin away from the flesh. Insert the truffle slices under the skin of the chicken and secure the skin firmly under the body. Mix together the Madeira, pâté and breadcrumbs, with salt and pepper to taste. Stuff the body of the chicken with the mixture, and truss.

Melt the butter in a roasting tin or flameproof casserole. Add the chicken and brown all over. Cover and transfer to a preheated moderately hot oven. Cook for 30 minutes, then reduce the heat to moderate. Continue cooking, basting frequently, for 1 hour or until the bird is golden and tender.

Transfer the chicken to a warmed serving platter and pour over the pan juices. Carve at the table. As this is a rich dish, serve with simple accompaniments such as freshly cooked seasonal vegetables.

31

Chicken with grapefruit

Metric	Imperial
50 g butter	2 oz butter
1 × 1.5 kg chicken	1 × 3 lb chicken
2 shallots, peeled and chopped	2 shallots, peeled and chopped
Salt	Salt
Pepper	Pepper
1 or 2 grapefruit, according to size	1 or 2 grapefruit, according to size
1 × 15 ml spoon sugar	1 tablespoon sugar

Cooking Time: About 1 hour 35 minutes
Oven: 200°C, 400°F, Gas Mark 6

Melt the butter in a roasting tin and add the chicken and shallots. Fry until lightly browned, then season with salt and pepper to taste. Transfer to a preheated moderately hot oven and roast for 1¼ hours.

Meanwhile, peel the rind from the grapefruit, being careful not to take any of the white pith with the rind, and cut it into very thin shreds. Blanch in boiling water for 3 minutes, then drain. Remove the pith from the grapefruit, then separate into segments. Peel the segments, if possible. Sprinkle with the sugar.

Transfer the chicken to a serving platter and keep hot. Pour the fat from the roasting tin, then put over heat on top of the stove. Stir in the fruit and shredded rind. Heat through gently. Serve the grapefruit mixture with the chicken.

Chicken with fresh pineapple

Metric	Imperial
1 × 1.75 kg chicken	1 × 3½ lb chicken
1 medium pineapple, peeled, cored and thinly sliced	1 medium pineapple, peeled, cored and thinly sliced
50 g butter	2 oz butter
2 shallots, peeled and chopped	2 shallots, peeled and chopped
Salt	Salt
Pepper	Pepper
Watercress to garnish	Watercress to garnish

Cooking Time: About 1¾ hours
Oven: 200°C, 400°F, Gas Mark 6

Lift the skin on the breast of the chicken by inserting your fingers from the neck end and gently easing the skin away from the flesh. Put a slice of pineapple under the skin on each breast of the chicken. Melt the butter in a roasting tin and add the shallots. Cook until softened. Add the chicken and brown lightly on all sides. Season with salt and pepper to taste, then transfer to a preheated moderately hot oven. Roast for 1 hour 20 minutes.

Transfer the chicken to a serving platter and keep hot. Add the remaining pineapple slices to the roasting tin and cook on top of the stove until the pineapple is heated through. Arrange around the chicken and garnish with watercress.

Chicken fines herbes

Metric	Imperial
50 g butter	2 oz butter
1 × 1.75 kg chicken, quartered or 4 chicken portions	1 × 3½ lb chicken, quartered or 4 chicken portions
100 g smoked bacon, rinds removed, finely diced	4 oz smoked bacon, rinds removed, finely diced
1 onion, peeled and chopped	1 onion, peeled and chopped
50 g plain flour	2 oz plain flour
600 ml chicken stock	1 pint chicken stock
1 × 15 ml spoon chopped fresh parsley	1 tablespoon chopped fresh parsley
1 × 15 ml spoon chopped fresh chives	1 tablespoon chopped fresh chives
1 × 15 ml spoon chopped fresh tarragon	1 tablespoon chopped fresh tarragon
1 × 15 ml spoon chopped fresh chervil	1 tablespoon chopped fresh chervil
Salt	Salt
Pepper	Pepper
2 × 15 ml spoons double cream	2 tablespoons double cream

Cooking Time: About 1¼ hours

Melt the butter in a flameproof casserole and add the chicken pieces, bacon and onion. Fry until the chicken pieces are lightly browned on all sides. Sprinkle over the flour and cook, stirring, for 1 minute. Stir in the stock. Bring to the boil and skim. Cover and simmer for 30 minutes.

Add 1.5 × 5 ml spoons (1½ teaspoons) of the parsley and all the remaining herbs. Cover and simmer for a further 20 minutes. Add salt and pepper to taste.

When the chicken is tender, stir in the cream and remaining parsley.

Chicken with grapefruit
Chicken fines herbes
Chicken with fresh pineapple

Right: Grilled chicken with warm aïoli
Centre right: Chicken with chestnuts
Far right: Grilled anchovy chicken

Grilled chicken with warm aïoli

Metric	Imperial
1 × 1.5 kg chicken, quartered or 4 chicken portions	1 × 3 lb chicken, quartered or 4 chicken portions
40 g butter, melted	1½ oz butter, melted
50 g plain flour	2 oz plain flour
Lemon wedges to garnish	Lemon wedges to garnish
Aïoli (Garlic mayonnaise):	Aïoli (Garlic mayonnaise):
2 egg yolks	2 egg yolks
Salt	Salt
Pepper	Pepper
15 g sugar	½ oz sugar
Juice of 1 lemon	Juice of 1 lemon
300 ml oil (preferably olive)	½ pint oil (preferably olive)
3 garlic cloves, crushed	3 garlic cloves, crushed
1 × 15 ml spoon boiling water	1 tablespoon boiling water

Cooking Time: 30–35 minutes

Brush the chicken with the melted butter, and dust with the flour. Cook under a preheated medium grill for 15 to 16 minutes on each side or until brown and tender.

Meanwhile, beat the egg yolks with salt and pepper to taste, the sugar and the lemon juice in a heatproof bowl. Gradually add the oil in drops, beating all the time until the mayonnaise thickens. When half the oil has been added, the remainder may be added in a thin stream. Mix in the garlic and stabilize the sauce by beating in the boiling water. Taste and adjust the seasoning. Stand the bowl in hot water to heat through gently.

Arrange the chicken on a warmed serving dish and coat with the warm mayonnaise. Garnish with lemon wedges.

Chicken with chestnuts

Metric	Imperial
500 g chestnuts	1 lb chestnuts
50 g butter	2 oz butter
1 × 1.5 kg chicken, quartered or 4 chicken portions	1 × 3 lb chicken, quartered or 4 chicken portions
2 onions, peeled and chopped	2 onions, peeled and chopped
600 ml chicken stock	1 pint chicken stock
50 g plain flour	2 oz plain flour
Salt	Salt
Pepper	Pepper
250 g button mushrooms	8 oz button mushrooms
Orange slices to garnish	Orange slices to garnish

Cooking Time: About 1½ hours

Cut the points off the chestnuts and put into a saucepan of cold water. Bring to the boil and simmer for 10 minutes. Drain and peel off both the outer and inner skins.

Melt the butter in a flameproof casserole. Add the chicken pieces and onions and fry until the chicken pieces are lightly browned on all sides. Meanwhile, poach the chestnuts in the stock for 25 minutes. Drain, reserving the stock.

Sprinkle the chicken with the flour and cook, stirring, for 1 minute. Add the stock from the chestnuts. Bring to the boil, stirring, and skim. Season with salt and pepper to taste and add the mushrooms. Cover and simmer for 1 hour.

Ten minutes before serving, add the chestnuts and heat through. Serve garnished with orange slices.

Grilled anchovy chicken

Metric

1 × 1.5 kg chicken,
quartered or 4 chicken
portions
40 g butter, melted
Salt
Pepper
50 g plain flour
Parsley sprigs to garnish

Sauce:
25 g butter
25 g plain flour
300 ml milk
2 × 15 ml spoons anchovy
essence
1 × 15 ml spoon tomato
purée
Juice of 1 lemon
1 × 50 g can anchovy
fillets, chopped

Imperial

1 × 3 lb chicken, quartered
or 4 chicken portions
1½ oz butter, melted
Salt
Pepper
2 oz plain flour
Parsley sprigs to garnish

Sauce:
1 oz butter
1 oz plain flour
½ pint milk
2 tablespoons anchovy
essence
1 tablespoon tomato purée
Juice of 1 lemon
1 × 2 oz can anchovy
fillets, chopped

Cooking Time: 30–35 minutes

Brush the chicken portions with the melted butter, season with salt and pepper, and dust with the flour. Cook under a preheated medium grill for 15 to 16 minutes on each side or until brown and tender. Keep hot.

To make the sauce, melt the butter in a saucepan. Add the flour and cook, stirring, for 1 minute. Gradually stir in the milk and bring to the boil, stirring. Simmer until thickened. Beat in the anchovy essence, tomato purée, lemon juice and anchovies with their oil. Heat through gently and add salt and pepper to taste.

Arrange the chicken pieces on a warmed serving dish and coat with the sauce. Garnish with parsley.

Chicken with bacon dumplings

Metric

1 × 15 ml spoon olive oil
1 × 1.75 kg chicken, cut
into small pieces
2 large onions, peeled and
chopped
1 garlic clove, crushed
25 g plain flour
600 ml chicken stock
1 bay leaf
Salt
Pepper

Dumplings:
225 g self-raising flour
Pinch of salt
25 g butter
100 g finely chopped suet
100 g streaky bacon, rinds
removed, minced or finely
chopped
1 small onion, peeled and
minced or finely chopped
Pinch of dried thyme
1 egg, beaten
Milk to moisten
900 ml chicken stock

Imperial

1 tablespoon olive oil
1 × 3½ lb chicken, cut into
small pieces
2 large onions, peeled and
chopped
1 garlic clove, crushed
1 oz plain flour
1 pint chicken stock
1 bay leaf
Salt
Pepper

Dumplings:
8 oz self-raising flour
Pinch of salt
1 oz butter
4 oz finely chopped suet
4 oz streaky bacon, rinds
removed, minced or finely
chopped
1 small onion, peeled and
minced or finely chopped
Pinch of dried thyme
1 egg, beaten
Milk to moisten
1½ pints chicken stock

Cooking Time: About 1¼ hours

Heat the oil in a flameproof casserole. Add the chicken, onions and garlic and fry until lightly browned. Sprinkle over the flour and cook, stirring, for 1 minute. Stir in the stock. Add the bay leaf and salt and pepper to taste. Simmer for 1 hour or until tender.

Meanwhile, for the dumplings, sift the flour and salt into a mixing bowl and rub in the butter. Mix in the suet, bacon, onion and thyme and moisten with the beaten egg and milk. Roll into small dumplings.

Bring the stock to the boil in another saucepan. Drop in the dumplings, cover and poach for 20 to 30 minutes or until they are puffed up and cooked through.

Transfer the dumplings to the chicken mixture, using a slotted spoon. Remove the bay leaf. Serve in the casserole.

Chicken with bacon dumplings; Chicken and mushroom pie

Chicken and mushroom pie

Metric

50 g butter
*1 × 1.75 kg chicken, cut
into 8 pieces*
*1 large onion, peeled and
chopped*
40 g plain flour
300 ml chicken stock
Salt
Pepper
1 bay leaf
175 g mushrooms, sliced
*225 g frozen puff pastry,
thawed*
1 egg, beaten

Imperial

2 oz butter
*1 × 3½ lb chicken, cut into
8 pieces*
*1 large onion, peeled and
chopped*
1½ oz plain flour
½ pint chicken stock
Salt
Pepper
1 bay leaf
6 oz mushrooms, sliced
*8 oz frozen puff pastry,
thawed*
1 egg, beaten

Cooking Time: About 2 hours
Oven: 200°C, 400°F, Gas Mark 6

Melt the butter in a saucepan. Add the chicken and onion
and fry until lightly browned. Sprinkle over the flour and
cook, stirring, for 1 minute. Stir in the stock. Bring to the
boil and skim. Add salt and pepper to taste and the bay leaf
and simmer for 1 hour or until the chicken is tender.
Remove the bay leaf. Allow to cool.
Stir in the mushrooms and transfer to a pie dish. Roll out
the dough and use to cover the dish. Make an airhole and
decorate with the pastry trimmings. Brush with the beaten
egg and bake in a preheated moderately hot oven for 40
minutes.

Boiling chickens

Boiling chickens should not be despised; they are merely a little older and have thus acquired more flavour. They do, of course, take longer to cook, and the length of time depends on the age of the bird. So test frequently after the first 2 hours simmering, and serve as soon as they are tender. Boilers can be as small as 1.5 kg (3 lb), but can weigh much more.

Boiled chicken with haricot beans

Metric	*Imperial*	Cooking Time: About 2 hours

1 × 1.75 kg boiler chicken
100 g dried haricot beans, soaked in cold water overnight and drained
1.75 l chicken stock
2 onions, peeled and quartered
2 garlic cloves, crushed
1 bay leaf
1 × 15 ml spoon dried tarragon
1 × 225 g can tomatoes
Salt
Pepper

1 × 3½ lb boiler chicken
4 oz dried haricot beans, soaked in cold water overnight and drained
3 pints chicken stock
2 onions, peeled and quartered
2 garlic cloves, crushed
1 bay leaf
1 tablespoon dried tarragon
1 × 8 oz can tomatoes
Salt
Pepper

Put the chicken and beans in a saucepan and add the stock. Bring to the boil and skim. Stir in the remaining ingredients with salt and pepper to taste. Cover and simmer for 2 hours or until the chicken is tender.
Transfer the chicken to a warmed serving dish and keep hot. Remove the bay leaf from the pan and sieve the bean mixture to form a smooth sauce. Alternatively, pass through a blender. Adjust the seasoning. Carve the chicken and serve with the bean sauce.

Far left: Boiled chicken with bacon collar
Left: Boiled chicken with rice
Above: Boiled chicken with haricot beans

Boiled chicken with bacon collar

Metric	Imperial
25 g butter	1 oz butter
2 onions, peeled and chopped	2 onions, peeled and chopped
3 celery stalks, chopped	3 celery stalks, chopped
2 carrots, peeled and chopped	2 carrots, peeled and chopped
1 × 2 kg boiler chicken	1 × 4 lb boiler chicken
1 × 1.75 kg piece collar of bacon, soaked in cold water overnight and drained	1 × 3½ lb piece collar of bacon, soaked in cold water overnight and drained
1 bay leaf	1 bay leaf
1 fresh thyme sprig	1 fresh thyme sprig
Salt	Salt
Pepper	Pepper
Watercress to garnish	Watercress to garnish

Cooking Time: 2-2½ hours

Melt the butter in a saucepan. Add the onions, celery and carrots and cook until softened. Add the chicken and bacon. Cover with water, bring to the boil and skim. Add the bay leaf, thyme and salt and pepper to taste. Simmer until cooked (test after 2 hours). If the bacon is done first, take it out and keep hot.

Remove the chicken and bacon from the pan. Return the stock to the heat and boil briskly to reduce while you carve the chicken and slice the bacon. Arrange the chicken and bacon on a warmed serving dish. Pour a little of the strained stock over as gravy and use the rest for soup. Garnish with watercress.
Serves 6 to 8

Boiled chicken with rice

Metric	Imperial
50 g butter	2 oz butter
2 onions, peeled and chopped	2 onions, peeled and chopped
2 celery stalks, chopped	2 celery stalks, chopped
1 × 2 kg boiler chicken with giblets	1 × 4 lb boiler chicken with giblets
Salt	Salt
Pepper	Pepper
1 bay leaf	1 bay leaf
175–225 g long-grain rice	6–8 oz long-grain rice
Chopped parsley to garnish	Chopped parsley to garnish

Cooking Time: 2½-3 hours

Melt the butter in a saucepan. Add the onions and celery and cook until softened. Add the chicken and its giblets, cover with water and bring to the boil. Skim. Season with salt and pepper to taste and add the bay leaf. Simmer gently for 2 to 2½ hours or until cooked.

Transfer the chicken to a serving platter and keep hot. Strain the cooking stock into another saucepan. Add the rice and cook until tender.

Meanwhile, chop the giblets, including any pickings from the neck. Drain the rice, if necessary, and stir in the giblet pieces. Adjust the seasoning, and serve round the carved chicken, garnished with parsley.

Boiled chicken and pasta

Metric	Imperial
50 g butter	2 oz butter
2 onions, peeled and chopped	2 onions, peeled and chopped
2 garlic cloves, crushed	2 garlic cloves, crushed
3 celery stalks, chopped	3 celery stalks, chopped
1 × 1.75 kg boiler chicken with giblets	1 × 3½ lb boiler chicken with giblets
Salt	Salt
Pepper	Pepper
1 bay leaf	1 bay leaf
1 × 15 ml spoon dried oregano	1 tablespoon dried oregano
175–225 g pasta (any favourite kind)	6–8 oz pasta (any favourite kind)
2 × 15 ml spoons olive oil	2 tablespoons olive oil
2 × 15 ml spoons grated Parmesan cheese	2 tablespoons grated Parmesan cheese
Tomato wedges to garnish	Tomato wedges to garnish

Cooking Time: 2½-3 hours

Melt the butter in a saucepan. Add the onions, garlic and celery and cook until softened. Add the chicken with its giblets, cover with water and bring to the boil. Skim. Season with salt and pepper to taste and add the bay leaf. Simmer gently for 2 to 2½ hours or until cooked.

Remove the chicken from the pan and allow to cool slightly, then remove the skin. Take the meat from the bones and dice it. Strain the cooking stock into another saucepan and add the oregano and pasta. Cook until tender.

Strain the stock back into the first saucepan, and reheat the chicken in this. Stir the olive oil into the pasta. Drain the hot chicken and pile on a warmed serving dish. Surround with the pasta and sprinkle over the Parmesan. Garnish with tomato wedges.

Boiled chicken con chilli

Metric	Imperial
3 × 15 ml spoons oil	3 tablespoons oil
1 × 1.5 kg boiler chicken, cut into 8 pieces	1 × 3 lb boiler chicken, cut into 8 pieces
2 onions, peeled and chopped	2 onions, peeled and chopped
3 garlic cloves, chopped	3 garlic cloves, chopped
2 × 15 ml spoons chilli powder or to taste	2 tablespoons chilli powder or to taste
600 ml chicken stock	1 pint chicken stock
1 × 225 g can tomatoes	1 × 8 oz can tomatoes
Salt	Salt
Pepper	Pepper
1 × 500 g can red kidney beans, rinsed and drained	1 × 1 lb can red kidney beans, rinsed and drained

Cooking Time: About 2¼ hours

This dish can be as hot and spicy as you choose, depending on how much chilli powder you use. Add it gradually, according to taste, remembering that some types of chilli are very hot.

Heat the oil in a flameproof casserole. Add the chicken pieces, onions and garlic and fry until lightly browned. Add the chilli powder (gradually) and fry gently for a further 2 minutes. Pour in the stock and the tomatoes with the can juice. Bring to the boil and skim. Add salt and pepper to taste. Simmer gently for about 2 hours or until tender.

Ten minutes before the chicken is ready, add the beans. Stir well and adjust the seasoning. (Alternatively, the beans may be heated and served separately.)

Boiled chicken and pasta;
Boiled chicken con chilli

Chicken soups

Cock-a-leekie

Metric

1 × 1.5 kg chicken
1.2 l chicken stock
1 bouquet garni
1 × 5 ml spoon dried
thyme
1 bay leaf
3 parsley stalks
50 g pearl barley
750 g leeks, sliced
225 g dried prunes,
soaked overnight and
drained
150–175 ml double cream
(to taste)
Salt
Pepper

Imperial

1 × 3 lb chicken
2 pints chicken stock
1 bouquet garni
1 teaspoon dried thyme
1 bay leaf
3 parsley stalks
2 oz pearl barley
1½ lb leeks, sliced
8 oz dried prunes, soaked
overnight and drained
5–6 fl oz double cream
(to taste)
Salt
Pepper

Cooking Time: About 1½ hours

This is, strictly speaking, a soup, but it is so substantial that it will make a main meal, served with bread.

Put the chicken, stock, bouquet garni, thyme, bay leaf, parsley and barley into a saucepan. Bring to the boil and simmer for 45 minutes. Add the leeks and continue cooking until the barley is cooked and the chicken is tender. Remove the chicken, bay leaf, parsley and bouquet garni and allow the chicken to cool.

Skin the bird. Take the meat from the bones and chop finely. Return the chicken meat to the soup, with the prunes, and simmer again until the prunes are tender. Stir in the cream and season with salt and pepper to taste.
Serves 6

Chicken broth

Metric

1 × 1.5 kg boiler chicken
Salt
Pepper
2 onions, peeled and
chopped
2 garlic cloves, crushed
2 carrots, peeled and
chopped
2 leeks, sliced
1 × 15 ml spoon dried
tarragon
3 celery stalks, chopped

Imperial

1 × 3 lb boiler chicken
Salt
Pepper
2 onions, peeled and
chopped
2 garlic cloves, crushed
2 carrots, peeled and
chopped
2 leeks, sliced
1 tablespoon dried
tarragon
3 celery stalks, chopped

Cooking Time: About 2¼ hours

Put the chicken into a large saucepan and cover with water. Bring to the boil and skim. Season with salt and pepper to taste. Cover and simmer for 1½ hours.

Add the remaining ingredients and bring back to the boil. Simmer for a further 45 minutes.

Remove the chicken from the pan and cut off the breasts. Skin and dice the meat finely and return to the broth. Adjust the seasoning and serve. Save the rest of the chicken for another dish, such as a salad (see pages 51–52).

Variations:
Chicken broth with vermicelli
Add 100 g (4 oz) vermicelli, broken into very small pieces, to the broth with the diced chicken meat and simmer for a further 5 minutes.
Chicken broth with barley
Thirty minutes before the broth has finished simmering, add 75 g (3 oz) pearl barley.

Cock-a-leekie;
Chicken broth

Chicken velouté soup

Metric	Imperial
1 × 1.5 kg boiler chicken	1 × 3 lb boiler chicken
2 onions, peeled and quartered	2 onions, peeled and quartered
2 garlic cloves, crushed	2 garlic cloves, crushed
2 carrots, peeled and sliced	2 carrots, peeled and sliced
2 leeks, sliced	2 leeks, sliced
2 celery stalks, chopped	2 celery stalks, chopped
1 × 15 ml spoon dried tarragon	1 tablespoon dried tarragon
75 g butter	3 oz butter
50 g plain flour	2 oz plain flour
Salt	Salt
Pepper	Pepper
2 egg yolks	2 egg yolks
120 ml double cream	4 fl oz double cream
1 × 15 ml spoon chopped fresh parsley to garnish	1 tablespoon chopped fresh parsley to garnish

Cooking Time: About 2 hours.

Put the chicken into a large saucepan and cover with water. Add the onions, garlic, carrots, leeks and celery. Bring to the boil and skim. Add the tarragon. Cover and simmer for 1½ hours or until the chicken is cooked.

Remove the chicken from the pan and cut off the breasts. Skin and dice the meat finely. Save the rest of the chicken for another dish (see pages 46–53). Strain the broth and reserve 1.8 l (3 pints).

Melt the butter in another saucepan and stir in the flour. Cook until the roux is a very pale straw colour. Stir in the reserved strained broth. Simmer until smooth and thickened, then add salt and pepper to taste. Beat together the egg yolks and cream. Remove the pan from the heat and beat in the egg yolk mixture. Return to the heat and heat through gently. Stir in the diced chicken breast and garnish with the parsley.

Variation:
Cream of chicken soup
Do not allow the butter and flour roux to colour (cook for only 1 minute). Omit the egg yolks and stir in the cream just before serving.

Chicken mulligatawny

Metric	Imperial
50 g plain flour	2 oz plain flour
1 × 15 ml spoon curry powder	1 tablespoon curry powder
40 g dripping	1½ oz dripping
1 onion, peeled and chopped	1 onion, peeled and chopped
4 streaky bacon rashers, rinds removed, minced	4 streaky bacon rashers, rinds removed, minced
225 g chicken pieces	8 oz chicken pieces
1.75 l water	3 pints water
1 × 5 ml spoon salt	1 teaspoon salt
Juice of ½ lemon	Juice of ½ lemon
1 × 5 ml spoon brown sugar	1 teaspoon brown sugar
Lemon slices to garnish	Lemon slices to garnish

Cooking Time: About 1¼ hours

Sift the flour and curry powder together. Melt the dripping in a saucepan and add the curry powder mixture. Fry, stirring, for 2 minutes. Add the onion, bacon and chicken and brown lightly. Add the water, bring to the boil and skim. Add the salt, lemon juice and sugar. Cover and simmer gently for 1 hour.

Remove the chicken pieces. Skin and chop the meat finely. Return to the pan and reheat. Adjust the seasoning. Serve with a lemon slice floating in each bowl.

Chicken and mushroom soup

Metric	Imperial
225 g chicken pieces	8 oz chicken pieces
1 onion, peeled and chopped	1 onion, peeled and chopped
1 garlic clove, crushed	1 garlic clove, crushed
1 × 5 ml spoon Worcestershire sauce	1 teaspoon Worcestershire sauce
225 g mushrooms, sliced	8 oz mushrooms, sliced
1 bay leaf	1 bay leaf
Salt	Salt
Pepper	Pepper
2 × 5 ml spoons arrowroot	2 teaspoons arrowroot
1 × 15 ml spoon water	1 tablespoon water
120 ml double cream	4 fl oz double cream

Cooking Time: About 1¼ hours

Put the chicken in a saucepan with the onion, garlic, Worcestershire sauce, mushrooms, bay leaf and water to cover. Bring to the boil and skim. Cover and simmer gently for 1 hour.

Remove the chicken and bay leaf. Skin and finely chop the meat. Season the broth with salt and pepper to taste. Dissolve the arrowroot in the water and add to the broth. Stir well and simmer for 5 minutes. Stir in the cream and chicken meat and heat through gently.

Chicken velouté soup

Chicken mulligatawny

Chicken and mushroom soup

Cold chicken dishes

Chicken breast in aspic

Metric	Imperial
1 × 2 kg boiler chicken, skinned	1 × 4 lb boiler chicken, skinned
1.75 l water	3 pints water
2 onions, peeled and stuck with 6 cloves	2 onions, peeled and stuck with 6 cloves
2 carrots, peeled and sliced	2 carrots, peeled and sliced
2 celery stalks, cut in short lengths	2 celery stalks, cut in short lengths
1 garlic clove, crushed	1 garlic clove, crushed
1 bay leaf	1 bay leaf
1 fresh thyme sprig	1 fresh thyme sprig
Salt	Salt
Pepper	Pepper
2 egg whites, crushed with their shells	2 egg whites, crushed with their shells
175 g minced lean leg of beef	6 oz minced lean leg of beef
4 × 15 ml spoons amontillado sherry	4 tablespoons amontillado sherry

To garnish:
Cucumber slices
Lettuce or watercress

Cooking Time: About 1 hour

With a sharp knife, remove the chicken breasts and cut each into two pieces lengthways. Chop up the rest of the chicken meat and put it in a saucepan with the water, onions, carrots, celery and garlic. Bring to the boil and skim. Add the herbs. As the liquid is going to be well reduced, be sparing with salt, but season well with pepper. Lay the breast pieces on top, cover and simmer for 30 minutes or until the breasts are tender when pierced with a skewer (the age of the bird determines the cooking time). Drain the chicken breast pieces and allow to cool.

Bring the liquid to the boil again and boil briskly until reduced to 600 ml (1 pint). Strain through muslin into another saucepan. Beat in the egg whites and beef. Bring slowly to the boil, then carefully strain through muslin again.

Arrange the chicken breast pieces in a 900 ml (1½ pint) capacity mould. Mix the sherry into the clarified stock and pour over the chicken. Chill until set, then turn out to serve. Garnish with cucumber slices and lettuce or watercress.

Chicken galantine

Metric	Imperial
1 × 1.5 kg boiler chicken, skinned	1 × 3 lb boiler chicken, skinned
1 × 15 ml spoon tomato purée	1 tablespoon tomato purée
1 × 5 ml spoon black pepper	1 teaspoon black pepper
1 × 5 ml spoon dried tarragon	1 teaspoon dried tarragon
1 × 5 ml spoon soy sauce	1 teaspoon soy sauce
1 × 5 ml spoon Worcestershire sauce	1 teaspoon Worcestershire sauce
1 egg, beaten	1 egg, beaten
120 ml dry white wine	4 fl oz dry white wine
Salt	Salt
750 g piece streaky bacon, rind removed	1½ lb piece streaky bacon, rind removed
2 bay leaves	2 bay leaves
75 g toasted white breadcrumbs	3 oz toasted white breadcrumbs
Parsley sprigs to garnish	Parsley sprigs to garnish

Cooking Time: 3 hours

With a sharp knife remove all the meat from the chicken that you can. Mince the chicken meat and add the tomato purée, pepper, tarragon, soy and Worcestershire sauces, egg, wine and salt to taste. Divide the mixture into two. Put one half on a greased sheet of greaseproof paper and shape into an oblong, about 5mm (¼ inch) thick.

Cut the bacon into long strips and arrange them lengthways on the chicken oblong. Cover with the rest of the chicken mixture. Put the bay leaves on top and roll up like a Swiss roll, using the paper to lift the mixture. Roll in a floured cloth and tie the ends. Put in a saucepan and cover with water. Bring to the boil and simmer for 3 hours.

Remove from the pan and allow to cool with a weight on top. When cold, chill overnight, still weighted.

Unwrap the next day and coat with the toasted breadcrumbs. Slice with a sharp knife to serve. Garnish with parsley.

Above: Chicken breast in aspic
Right: Chicken galantine

Savoury chicken loaf

Metric

1 × 1.5 kg boiler chicken, skinned
100 g streaky bacon rashers, rinds removed, minced
225 g beef sausagemeat
1 onion, peeled and minced
1 × 5 ml spoon dried mixed herbs
2 garlic cloves, crushed
100 ml dry cider
2 bay leaves

Imperial

1 × 3 lb boiler chicken, skinned
4 oz streaky bacon rashers, rinds removed, minced
8 oz beef sausagemeat
1 onion, peeled and minced
1 teaspoon dried mixed herbs
2 garlic cloves, crushed
3 fl oz dry cider
2 bay leaves

Cooking Time: 2½ hours
Oven: 160°C, 325°F, Gas Mark 3

Remove the meat from the chicken and mince it. Mix well with the bacon, sausagemeat, onion, herbs, garlic and cider. Turn into a well-greased 1 kg (2 lb) loaf tin, put the bay leaves on top and cover with foil. Bake in a preheated moderate oven for 2½ hours. Allow to cool, and chill before slicing.

Chicken pâté de campagne

Metric

1 × 1.5 kg boiler chicken, skinned
100 g chicken livers
225 g streaky bacon rashers, rinds removed, minced
1 × 15 ml spoon dried tarragon
1 onion, peeled and minced
2 garlic cloves, crushed
1 × 15 ml spoon tomato purée
150 ml dry red wine
Salt
Pepper
1 × 5 ml spoon dried thyme
2 bay leaves

To garnish:
Lettuce leaves
Tomato slices

Imperial

1 × 3 lb boiler chicken, skinned
4 oz chicken livers
8 oz streaky bacon rashers, rinds removed, minced
1 tablespoon dried tarragon
1 onion, peeled and minced
2 garlic cloves, crushed
1 tablespoon tomato purée
¼ pint dry red wine
Salt
Pepper
1 teaspoon dried thyme
2 bay leaves

To garnish:
Lettuce leaves
Tomato slices

Cooking Time: 2½ hours
Oven: 150°C, 300°F, Gas Mark 2

Remove the meat from the chicken and mince it coarsely with the chicken livers. Mix with the bacon, tarragon, onion, garlic, tomato purée, wine, salt and pepper to taste and the thyme. Turn into a well-greased terrine, put the bay leaves on top and cover. Bake in a preheated warm oven for 2½ hours. Cool and chill before serving, garnished with lettuce and tomato.

Chicken mousse

Metric

1 × 70 g packet aspic jelly powder
600 ml chicken stock
500 g cooked chicken meat, shredded
100 ml dry sherry
1 × 5 ml spoon dried tarragon
Pepper
300 ml double cream
2 × 5 ml spoons tomato purée
Watercress to garnish

Imperial

1 × 2½ oz packet aspic jelly powder
1 pint chicken stock
1 lb cooked chicken meat, shredded
3 fl oz dry sherry
1 teaspoon dried tarragon
Pepper
½ pint double cream
2 teaspoons tomato purée
Watercress to garnish

Make up the aspic with the stock, according to the instructions on the packet. Allow to cool until on the point of setting. Put the aspic, with the chicken, sherry, tarragon and a little pepper into a blender goblet and blend until smooth. Beat in the cream and tomato purée and turn into a dampened 1.5 l (2½ pint) capacity mould. Chill until set. Turn out to serve, garnished with watercress.

Top left: Chicken pâté de campagne
Top right: Savoury chicken loaf
Right: Chicken mousse

Chicken and sweetcorn salad

Metric	Imperial
225 g cooked chicken meat, shredded	8 oz cooked chicken meat, shredded
1 × 15 ml spoon soy sauce	1 tablespoon soy sauce
1 × 500 g can sweetcorn, drained	1 × 1 lb can sweetcorn, drained
Salt	Salt
Pepper	Pepper
Lettuce leaves	Lettuce leaves

Marinate the chicken in the soy sauce for 30 minutes. Mix well with the sweetcorn and season to taste with salt and pepper. Line a salad bowl with lettuce leaves and pile the chicken mixture in the centre.

Chicken and green pepper salad

Metric	Imperial
225 g cooked chicken meat, shredded	8 oz cooked chicken meat, shredded
4 × 15 ml spoons Vinaigrette Dressing (see page 68)	4 tablespoons Vinaigrette Dressing (see page 68)
1 large green pepper, cored, seeded and thinly sliced	1 large green pepper, cored, seeded and thinly sliced
275 g cold cooked rice	10 oz cold cooked rice
Salt	Salt
Pepper	Pepper

Marinate the chicken in the vinaigrette dressing for 10 minutes, then mix with the green pepper and rice. Season to taste with salt and pepper and leave in a cool place, loosely covered, for 1 hour before serving.

Tarragon chaudfroid of chicken

Metric	Imperial
1 × 1.75 kg chicken	1 × 3½ lb chicken
Salt	Salt
Pepper	Pepper
1 bunch of fresh tarragon	1 bunch of fresh tarragon
25 g butter, melted	1 oz butter, melted
2 egg yolks	2 egg yolks
Juice of 1½ lemons	Juice of 1½ lemons
1 × 5 ml spoon sugar	1 teaspoon sugar
300 ml olive oil	½ pint olive oil
1 × 70 g packet aspic jelly powder	1 × 2½ oz packet aspic jelly powder
450 ml water	¾ pint water

Cooking Time: About 1½ hours
Oven: 200°C, 400°F, Gas Mark 6

Season the chicken with salt and pepper, and stuff the body with the tarragon, reserving a few sprigs for garnish. Truss the bird and brush with the melted butter. Place in a roasting tin and roast in a preheated moderately hot oven for 1 hour 20 minutes. Allow to cool.

Meanwhile, make a mayonnaise with the egg yolks, lemon juice, sugar, a little salt and pepper and the olive oil (see page 34).

Make up the aspic with the water, according to the directions on the packet. (This quantity of water will produce a stiffer aspic than usual.) Allow the aspic jelly to cool, almost to setting.

Skin the chicken and cut into attractive serving pieces, i.e. two breast pieces, two thigh pieces, and two wings. Beat all but 4 × 15 ml spoons (4 tablespoons) of the aspic into the mayonnaise and use to coat the chicken pieces. Chill until set.

Blanch the remaining tarragon in boiling water for 2 minutes, then immediatly refresh in cold water. Decorate the chicken pieces with the blanched tarragon, and glaze with the reserved aspic. Chill again until set.

Chicken and sweetcorn salad;
Chicken and green pepper salad;
Tarragon chaudfroid of chicken

Chicken, lettuce and tomato salad

Metric	Imperial
3 × 15 ml spoons thick mayonnaise	*3 tablespoons thick mayonnaise*
225 g cooked chicken meat, shredded	*8 oz cooked chicken meat, shredded*
4 tomatoes, skinned and sliced	*4 tomatoes, skinned and sliced*
1 crisp lettuce, torn into small pieces	*1 crisp lettuce, torn into small pieces*

Mix the mayonnaise with the chicken. Arrange the tomatoes and lettuce on a serving platter and pile the chicken mixture on top.

Chicken and noodle salad

Metric	Imperial
4 × 15 ml spoons oil	*4 tablespoons oil*
225 g cooked chicken meat, shredded	*8 oz cooked chicken meat, shredded*
Salt	*Salt*
Pepper	*Pepper*
350 g cold cooked noodles	*12 oz cold cooked noodles*
75 g Parmesan cheese, grated	*3 oz Parmesan cheese, grated*
Watercress to garnish	*Watercress to garnish*

Mix 1 × 15 ml spoon (1 tablespoon) of the oil with the chicken and season with salt and pepper to taste. Toss the noodles in the remaining oil and mix together with the chicken. Spoon into a serving dish and sprinkle with the grated cheese. Garnish with watercress.

Chicken, lettuce and tomato salad; Chicken and noodle salad;
Chicken, orange and rice salad

Chicken, orange and rice salad

Metric

225 g cooked chicken
meat, shredded
275 g cold cooked rice
1 × 275 g can mandarin
orange segments, drained
4 × 15 ml spoons oil
Salt
Pepper
Chopped parsley to
garnish

Imperial

8 oz cooked chicken
meat, shredded
10 oz cold cooked rice
1 × 10 oz can mandarin
orange segments, drained
4 tablespoons oil
Salt
Pepper
Chopped parsley to
garnish

Mix all the ingredients together with salt and pepper to
taste. Sprinkle over the parsley and serve.

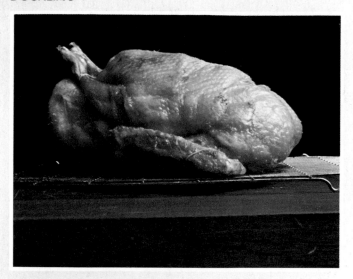

DUCKLING

Against the incomparable flavour of a duckling must be set the disadvantage that there is not much on the breast and a duckling of 1 to 1.5 kg (2 to 3 lb) will only just serve two people. Larger ducklings, or the older ducks, can, indeed, be carved, but considerable skill is required, so it is best to joint, say, a 2 kg (4 lb) bird into four pieces. The giblets of a duckling are very valuable as the long neck lends itself to stocks for soups and pies, while the large tender liver is of excellent flavour, and pâtés and many other delicious dishes may be made from it. A duckling, before roasting, should be pricked all over to allow the fat, of which there is a great deal, to escape.
To test if a duckling is cooked, pierce the thigh with a skewer: the juices that run out should be clear.

Roast duckling

Metric	Imperial
1 × 1.75–2 kg duckling	1 × 3½–4 lb duckling
Salt	Salt
Pepper	Pepper

Above: Roast duckling
Below: Roast stuffed duckling
Far right: Duckling with grapefruit

Cooking Time: 1 hour 10–20 minutes
Oven: 200°C, 400°F, Gas Mark 6

Put the duckling on a rack in a roasting tin. Prick the skin of the bird all over with a sharp skewer, then rub with salt and pepper. Roast in a preheated moderately hot oven for 1 hour 10 to 20 minutes or until cooked. There is no need to baste.

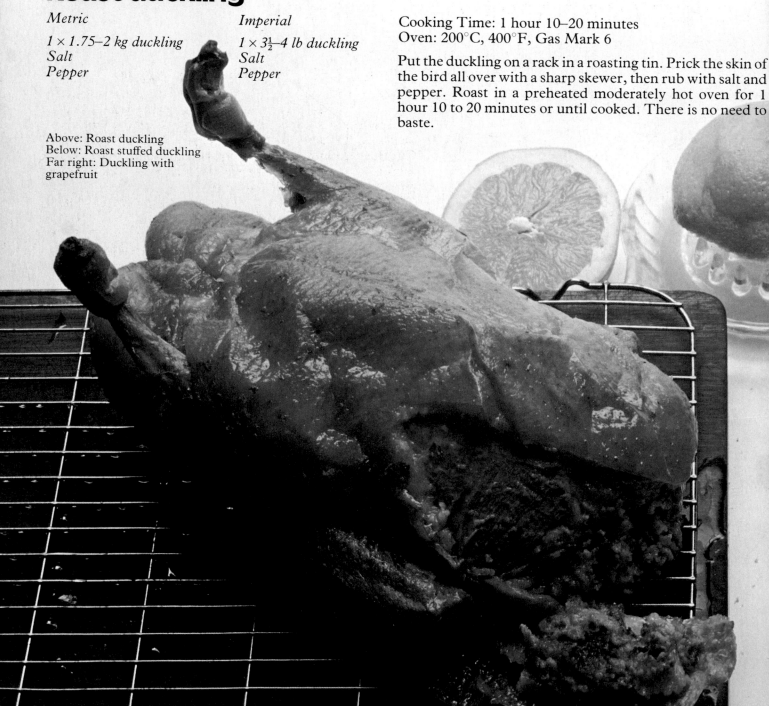

Roast stuffed duckling

Metric	Imperial
1 × 1.75–2 kg duckling	1 × 3½–4 lb duckling
Orange wedges to garnish	Orange wedges to garnish
Stuffing:	Stuffing:
100 g fresh white breadcrumbs	4 oz fresh white breadcrumbs
Duck liver, minced	Duck liver, minced
Juice and grated rind of 1 orange	Juice and grated rind of 1 orange
1 × 2.5 ml spoon dried sage	½ teaspoon dried sage
1 shallot, peeled and finely chopped	1 shallot, peeled and finely chopped
1 small egg, beaten	1 small egg, beaten
Salt	Salt
Pepper	Pepper

Cooking Time: 1½ hours
Oven: 200°C, 400°F, Gas Mark 6

Mix all the stuffing ingredients well together with salt and pepper to taste and stuff the duckling at the neck. Tuck the neck flap well under the bird and sew or skewer in place. Prick the skin. Place on a rack in a roasting tin. Roast in a preheated moderately hot oven for 1½ hours or until cooked. Serve garnished with orange wedges.

Duckling with grapefruit

Metric	Imperial
1 × 2 kg duckling	1 × 4 lb duckling
Salt	Salt
Pepper	Pepper
1 large grapefruit	1 large grapefruit

Cooking Time: About 1½ hours
Oven: 200°C, 400°F, Gas Mark 6

Put the duckling on a rack in a roasting tin. Prick all over and rub with salt and pepper. Roast in a preheated moderately hot oven for 1 hour 20 minutes or until cooked. Meanwhile, remove the rind from half the grapefruit, being careful not to take any of the white pith with the rind. Cut the rind into slivers and blanch in boiling water for 3 minutes. Drain. Peel the grapefruit, removing all the white pith, and separate into segments.

When the duckling is done, joint it and keep hot on a warmed serving platter. Pour off most of the fat and juices from the roasting tin and put over a low heat on top of the stove. Add the grapefruit segments and shredded rind and heat through gently.

To serve, arrange the grapefruit segments round the duckling and pour the tin juices over.

Duckling aux raisins

Metric

1 × 2 kg duckling
Salt
Pepper
300 ml pure grape juice
225 g white grapes,
halved and pitted

Imperial

1 × 4 lb duckling
Salt
Pepper
½ pint pure grape juice
8 oz white grapes, halved
and pitted

Cooking Time: About 1½ hours
Oven: 200°C, 400°F, Gas Mark 6

The sauce for this dish is thin and delicate in flavour.
Put the duckling on a rack in a roasting tin. Prick all over
and rub with salt and pepper. Roast in a preheated
moderately hot oven for 1 hour 20 minutes or until cooked.
After 1 hour, pour off most of the fat and juices from the tin
and baste the bird with the grape juice. When the duckling
is cooked, joint it and arrange on a warmed serving platter.
Keep hot.
Skim the fat from the roasting tin. Put the tin over low heat
on top of the stove. Add the grapes and heat through
gently. Pour the grape sauce over the duckling and serve.

Duckling aux cerises

Metric

1 × 2 kg duckling
Salt
Pepper
1 × 500 g can Morello
cherries
4 × 15 ml spoons kirsch

Imperial

1 × 4 lb duckling
Salt
Pepper
1 × 1 lb can Morello
cherries
4 tablespoons kirsch

Cooking Time: About 1½ hours
Oven: 200°C, 400°F, Gas Mark 6

Put the duckling on a rack in a roasting tin. Prick all over
and rub with salt and pepper. Roast in a preheated
moderately hot oven for 1 hour 20 minutes or until cooked.
After 1 hour, pour off most of the fat and juices from the tin
and continue to roast, basting the duckling with the syrup
from the can of cherries every 10 minutes.
When the duckling is done, joint it and keep hot on a
warmed serving platter. Put the roasting tin over low heat
on top of the stove and add the cherries. Heat through
gently.
Garnish the duckling with the hot cherries. Stir the kirsch
into the tin, then pour this sauce over the duckling.

Duckling au citron

Metric

1 × 2 kg duckling
Salt
Pepper
2 lemons
50 g sugar
2 × 15 ml spoons water
4 × 15 ml spoons gin
Watercress to garnish

Imperial

1 × 4 lb duckling
Salt
Pepper
2 lemons
2 oz sugar
2 tablespoons water
4 tablespoons gin
Watercress to garnish

Cooking Time: About 1½ hours
Oven: 200°C, 400°F, Gas Mark 6

Put the duckling on a rack in a roasting tin. Prick all over
and rub with salt and pepper. Roast in a preheated
moderately hot oven for 1 hour 20 minutes or until cooked.
Meanwhile, remove the rind from one of the lemons, being
careful not to take any of the white pith with the rind. Cut
the rind into slivers. Peel both lemons, removing all the
white pith, and separate into segments.
Put the sugar and water in a saucepan and stir over low heat
to dissolve the sugar. Bring to the boil and boil until
caramelized to a golden brown. Remove from the heat and
add the lemon segments and shredded rind.
When the duckling is ready, joint it and place on a warmed
serving dish. Surround with the caramelized lemon
segments and keep hot.
Pour off most of the fat and juices from the roasting tin and
place over low heat on top of the stove. Add the caramel
and lemon rind mixture and gin and heat through gently.
Pour over the duckling and serve, garnished with
watercress.
Note: if lemon gin is available, use it instead of ordinary
gin.

Duckling aux raisins

Duckling aux cerises

Duckling au citron

Duckling à l'orange

Metric	Imperial
1 × 2 kg duckling	1 × 4 lb duckling
Salt	Salt
Pepper	Pepper
300 ml unsweetened orange juice	½ pint unsweetened orange juice
4 small oranges	4 small oranges
4 × 15 ml spoons orange-flavoured liqueur	4 tablespoons orange-flavoured liqueur

Cooking Time: About 1½ hours
Oven: 200°C, 400°F, Gas Mark 6

Put the duckling on a rack in a roasting tin and prick all over. Rub with salt and pepper. Roast in a preheated moderately hot oven for 1 hour 20 minutes or until cooked. After 1 hour, pour off almost all the fat and juices from the tin and baste the bird with the orange juice.

Remove the rind from two of the oranges, being careful not to take any of the white pith with the rind. Cut the rind into slivers and blanch in boiling water for 3 minutes. Drain. Peel all the oranges, removing the white pith, and separate into segments.

When the duckling is done, joint it and keep hot on a warmed serving platter. Place the tin over low heat on top of the stove and add the orange segments and shredded rind. Heat through gently.

Arrange the orange segments around the duckling. Stir the liqueur into the tin, then pour this sauce over the duckling.

Duckling à l'orange; Duckling rouennais

Duckling rouennais

Metric

2 × 1.5 kg ducklings
with giblets
1 onion, peeled and
quartered
2 carrots, peeled and
halved
2 celery stalks
2 bay leaves
1 × 15 ml spoon tomato
purée
300 ml dry red wine
300 ml water
Salt
Pepper
40 g butter
25 g plain flour
100 ml port wine

Imperial

2 × 3 lb ducklings with
giblets
1 onion, peeled and
quartered
2 carrots, peeled and
halved
2 celery stalks
2 bay leaves
1 tablespoon tomato purée
½ pint dry red wine
½ pint water
Salt
Pepper
1½ oz butter
1 oz plain flour
3 fl oz port wine

Cooking Time: About 1½ hours
Oven: 220°C, 425°F, Gas Mark 7

Put the duckling giblets (reserving the liver), onion,
carrots, celery, bay leaves, tomato purée, wine and water
into a saucepan and bring to the boil. Simmer for 1 hour,
skimming when necessary. Add salt and pepper to taste,
then strain the stock.

Meanwhile, put the ducklings on a rack in a roasting tin
and prick all over. Roast in a preheated hot oven for 45
minutes. Remove from the oven and cut off the legs. Keep
the rest of the duckling warm. Score the legs and finish
cooking them under a preheated moderate grill for 20
minutes.

Melt the butter in another saucepan and add the flour.
Cook, stirring, for 1 minute, then gradually stir in the
strained stock. Simmer, stirring, until smooth and thickened. Put the sauce in a blender with the raw duck liver
and the port. Blend until smooth. Adjust the seasoning.

Slice the duckling breasts thinly. Serve a leg and as much
breast as possible to each guest and hand the sauce
separately.

Cold duckling dishes

All the following dishes are made with cold roast duckling as a base. Roast a 1.5–2 kg (3–4 lb) duckling in a preheated moderately hot oven (200°C, 400°F, Gas Mark 6) for 1 hour 10 to 20 minutes, as in the basic recipe on page 55. Allow to cool, then remove the skin and proceed as each recipe indicates.

Duckling pâté

Metric

150 g butter
1 duckling's liver
2 shallots, peeled and chopped
1 × 1.5 kg cold roast duckling, boned
Grated rind and juice of 1 orange
4 × 15 ml spoons port wine
Pinch of powdered bay
Pinch of dried rosemary
Salt
Pepper

Imperial

5 oz butter
1 duckling's liver
2 shallots, peeled and chopped
1 × 3 lb cold roast duckling, boned
Grated rind and juice of 1 orange
4 tablespoons port wine
Pinch of powdered bay
Pinch of dried rosemary
Salt
Pepper

Melt 15 g ($\frac{1}{2}$ oz) of the butter in a saucepan. Add the liver and fry quickly until lightly browned on both sides. Remove from the pan and allow to cool. Melt a further 15 g ($\frac{1}{2}$ oz) butter in the pan. Add the shallots and cook gently until soft but not brown.
Pass the liver, shallots, duckling and 75 g (3 oz) of the remaining butter through the fine blade of a mincer twice. Mix together well.
Stir in the orange rind and juice, port, herbs and salt and pepper to taste. Put into a terrine and seal with the remaining butter, melted. Leave in the refrigerator overnight to set before serving.

Duckling en gelée

Metric

1 × 1.75–2 kg cold roast duckling, cut into small pieces and boned
1 × 70 g packet aspic jelly powder
450 ml water
100 ml amontillado sherry
Lettuce leaves

Imperial

1 × 3$\frac{1}{2}$–4 lb cold roast duckling, cut into small pieces and boned
1 × 2$\frac{1}{2}$ oz packet aspic jelly powder
$\frac{3}{4}$ pint water
3 fl oz amontillado sherry
Lettuce leaves

Pack the duckling pieces neatly into a shallow dish. Make up the aspic with the water and sherry, according to the directions on the packet. Allow to cool until on the point of setting. Pour over the duckling. Chill until set.
Line a serving plate with lettuce leaves and turn out the jellied duckling onto it.

Far left: Duckling pâté
Left: Duckling en gelée
Right: Duckling mousse

Duckling mousse

Metric	Imperial
25 g butter	1 oz butter
1 duckling's liver, chopped	1 duckling's liver, chopped
2 shallots, peeled and chopped	2 shallots, peeled and chopped
1 × 70 g packet aspic jelly powder	1 × 2½ oz packet aspic jelly powder
500 ml water	1 pint water
1 × 1.5 kg cold roast duckling, boned and diced	1 × 3 lb cold roast duckling, boned and diced
100 ml port wine	3 fl oz port wine
150 ml double cream	¼ pint double cream
2 egg yolks	2 egg yolks
1 × 5 ml spoon dried tarragon	1 teaspoon dried tarragon
1 × 15 ml spoon tomato purée	1 tablespoon tomato purée
Grated rind and juice of 1 orange	Grated rind and juice of 1 orange
Salt	Salt
Pepper	Pepper
Orange slices to garnish	Orange slices to garnish

Melt 15 g (½ oz) of the butter in a saucepan. Add the liver and fry quickly until lightly browned on all sides. Remove from the pan and allow to cool. Melt the remaining butter in the pan. Add the shallots and cook gently until soft but not brown. Remove from the heat.

Make up the aspic with the water, according to the directions on the packet. Cool.

Put the liver, shallots, diced duckling, aspic, port wine, cream, egg yolks, tarragon, tomato purée and orange rind and juice in a blender goblet. Blend until very smooth. Season with salt and pepper to taste and turn into a 1.2 l (2 pint) capacity mould. Chill until set. Turn out to serve, garnished with orange slices.

Duckling, orange and rice salad

Metric	Imperial
2 egg yolks	2 egg yolks
1 × 175 g can mandarin orange segments	1 × 6 oz can mandarin orange segments
Salt	Salt
Pepper	Pepper
175 ml oil	6 fl oz oil
275 g cold cooked rice	10 oz cold cooked rice
350 g cold roast duckling meat, shredded	12 oz cold roast duckling meat, shredded

Beat the egg yolks with about 3 × 15 ml spoons (3 tablespoons) of the syrup from the oranges to flavour. Add salt and pepper to taste and the oil to make an orange-flavoured mayonnaise (see page 34). If the mayonnaise is really thick, add more of the syrup to thin it. Mix the drained oranges with the rice and duckling and lightly fold in the mayonnaise.

Duckling, green pepper and green pea salad

Metric	Imperial
350 g cold roast duckling meat, shredded	12 oz cold roast duckling meat, shredded
225 g green peas, cooked	8 oz green peas, cooked
1 large green pepper, cored, seeded and chopped	1 large green pepper, cored, seeded and chopped
3 × 15 ml spoons Vinaigrette Dressing (see page 68)	3 tablespoons Vinaigrette Dressing (see page 68)
1 × 15 ml spoon chopped fresh mint	1 tablespoon chopped fresh mint

Mix together the duckling, peas, green pepper and dressing and sprinkle with the mint. Allow to stand for 1 hour before serving.

Duckling, pasta and cheese salad

Metric	Imperial
350 g cooked pasta	12 oz cooked pasta
2 × 15 ml spoons oil	2 tablespoons oil
350 g cold roast duckling meat, shredded	12 oz cold roast duckling meat, shredded
150 g Parmesan cheese, grated	5 oz Parmesan cheese, grated
Salt	Salt
Pepper	Pepper
Chopped parsley to garnish	Chopped parsley to garnish

Toss the pasta with the oil, then fold in the remaining ingredients with salt and pepper to taste. Add more oil if necessary. Sprinkle with parsley before serving.

Duckling, orange and rice salad; Duckling, pasta and cheese salad; Duckling, green pepper and green pea salad

GOOSE

That unhappy lady, Queen Caroline, albeit a great trencher-woman, was heard to pronounce: 'The goose is an unsatisfactory bird; it's too much for one, and not enough for two.' Although this seems preposterous, one can see her point. For its size, there is relatively little meat on a goose, so allow 350 g (12 oz) of raw goose per person.

The goose should have enough fat on its body, so that basting is not necessary. To test if a goose is cooked, pierce the thigh with a skewer: the juices that run out should be clear.

Roast stuffed goose

Metric

1 × 5.5 kg goose
Fresh herbs to garnish

Stuffing:
40 g butter
1 onion, peeled and finely
chopped
Goose liver
350 g fresh white
breadcrumbs
1 × 5 ml spoon dried sage
1 × 5 ml spoon dried
mixed herbs
100 g chopped suet
2 eggs, beaten
Goose or chicken stock
Salt
Pepper

Imperial

1 × 12 lb goose
Fresh herbs to garnish

Stuffing:
1½ oz butter
1 onion, peeled and finely
chopped
Goose liver
12 oz fresh white
breadcrumbs
1 teaspoon dried sage
1 teaspoon dried mixed
herbs
4 oz chopped suet
2 eggs, beaten
Goose or chicken stock
Salt
Pepper

Cooking Time: 3¾ hours
Oven: 200°C, 400°F, Gas Mark 6

It is always better to stuff a goose at the neck as the flavour gets into the breast, and the stuffing is more thoroughly cooked.

Melt the butter in a frying pan and add the onion and goose liver. Cook gently until the onion is soft but not brown and the liver is lightly browned on both sides. Remove from the heat and chop the liver. Mix together the remaining stuffing ingredients, with stock to moisten and salt and pepper to taste, and add the onion and liver.

Stuff the neck end of the goose. Pull the neck flap well under the body of the bird and either sew or skewer it. Place in a roasting tin. Cover loosely with a sheet of foil and roast in a preheated moderately hot oven for 3¾ hours. Garnish the serving platter with a bunch of fresh herbs.

Serves 10 to 12

Roast goose

Metric

1 × 5.5 kg goose
Salt
Pepper

Imperial

1 × 12 lb goose
Salt
Pepper

Cooking Time: 3¼ hours
Oven: 200°C, 400°F, Gas Mark 6

Take the fat from the body of the goose and spread it over the breast. Place the goose in a roasting tin. Season with salt and pepper and cover loosely with a sheet of foil. Roast in a preheated moderately hot oven for 3¼ hours.

Serves 10

Left: Roast stuffed goose
Right: Roast goose

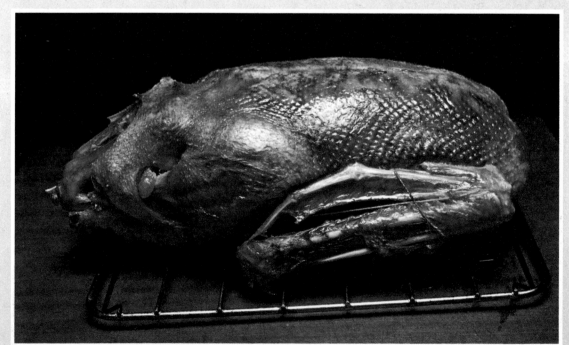

Cold goose dishes

Goose pâté de campagne

Metric

1 × 2.75 kg goose, skinned and boned
175 g bacon, rind removed
Goose liver
2 onions, peeled and finely chopped
2 garlic cloves, crushed
1 × 15 ml spoon tomato purée
150 ml dry red wine
1 × 5 ml spoon dried thyme
Salt
Pepper
2 bay leaves
100 ml brandy

Imperial

1 × 6 lb goose, skinned and boned
6 oz bacon, rind removed
Goose liver
2 onions, peeled and finely chopped
2 garlic cloves, crushed
1 tablespoon tomato purée
¼ pint dry red wine
1 teaspoon dried thyme
Salt
Pepper
2 bay leaves
3 fl oz brandy

Cooking Time: 3½ hours
Oven: 160°C, 325°F, Gas Mark 3

Mince the goose meat coarsely with plenty of goose fat, the bacon and goose liver. Mix in the onions, garlic, tomato purée, red wine, thyme and salt and pepper to taste. Turn into a well-greased terrine. Put the bay leaves on top and cover.

Bake in a preheated moderate oven for about 3½ hours. Cool under a weighted plate and chill overnight, still weighted. Remove the bay leaves and pour over the brandy. Leave for 30 minutes to permeate before serving.

Serves 8 to 10

Goose pâté de campagne; Goose breast in aspic;
St. Clement's goose salad

Goose breast in aspic

Metric	Imperial
1 × 5.5 kg cold roast goose	1 × 12 lb cold roast goose
3 red dessert apples, cored and thinly sliced	3 red dessert apples, cored and thinly sliced
1 × 70 g packet aspic jelly powder	1 × 2½ oz packet aspic jelly powder
600 ml medium cider	1 pint medium cider

Skin and slice the breast of goose neatly and arrange on a shallow dish. Strip the meat from the legs and carcass and shred it for use in salads. Dip the apple slices in salted water to keep their colour. Arrange these on the goose breast.
Make up the aspic with the cider, according to the directions on the packet. Allow to cool until on the point of setting. Pour over the goose and chill until set.
Serves 8

St. Clement's goose salad

Metric	Imperial
2 oranges, peeled and segmented	2 oranges, peeled and segmented
2 × 15 ml spoons raisins	2 tablespoons raisins
Juice of 2 lemons	Juice of 2 lemons
2 ripe avocados, peeled, stoned and sliced	2 ripe avocados, peeled, stoned and sliced
275 g cold roast goose meat, skinned and shredded	10 oz cold roast goose meat, skinned and shredded
Salt and pepper	Salt and pepper

Marinate the orange segments and raisins in the lemon juice for 1 hour. Fold in the avocado slices. Season the goose with salt and pepper to taste and add to the avocado mixture.

67

Goose and celery salad

Metric	Imperial
275 g cold roast goose meat, skinned and shredded	10 oz cold roast goose meat, skinned and shredded
4 × 15 ml spoons Vinaigrette Dressing (see below)	4 tablespoons Vinaigrette Dressing (see below)
1 crisp lettuce, separated into leaves	1 crisp lettuce, separated into leaves
½ head of celery, chopped	½ head of celery, chopped
100 g walnuts, chopped	4 oz walnuts, chopped

Mix together the goose meat and dressing and leave to marinate for 1 hour.
Arrange the lettuce leaves in a salad bowl.
Add the celery and walnuts and pile
the goose on top.

Goose and red cabbage salad

Metric	Imperial
225 g red cabbage, cored, shredded, blanched for 2 minutes and refreshed in cold water	8 oz red cabbage, cored, shredded, blanched for 2 minutes and refreshed in cold water
275 g cold roast goose meat, skinned and shredded	10 oz cold roast goose meat, skinned and shredded
1 × 5 ml spoon caraway seeds	1 teaspoon caraway seeds
Vinaigrette dressing:	Vinaigrette dressing:
150 ml oil	¼ pint oil
Juice of 1 lemon	Juice of 1 lemon
Salt	Salt
Pepper	Pepper

Put the ingredients for the dressing, with salt and pepper to taste, in a screwtop jar and shake until well mixed. Pour over the well-drained cabbage and leave to marinate for 1 hour. Fold in the goose and caraway seeds and serve.

Goose salad with rice

Metric	Imperial
275 g cold roast goose meat, skinned and shredded	10 oz cold roast goose meat, skinned and shredded
350 g cold cooked long-grain rice	12 oz cold cooked long-grain rice
225 g mushrooms, sliced	8 oz mushrooms, sliced
6–8 spring onions, including green part, sliced	6–8 spring onions, including green part, sliced
1 × 15 ml spoon Worcestershire sauce	1 tablespoon Worcestershire sauce
150 ml oil	¼ pint oil
Juice of 1 lemon	Juice of 1 lemon
Salt	Salt
Pepper	Pepper

Mix all the ingredients together, with salt and pepper to taste, and allow to stand for 1 hour, tossing from time to time.

Far left: Goose and celery salad
Left: Goose salad with rice
Below: Goose and red cabbage salad

TURKEY

Everyone seems to have a theory about how to roast a turkey. Some nervous extremists put the turkey in the oven the night before, while others think they can rush it through the cooking like a meringue topping. It seems better to fall between these two and to time the cooking according to a well worked-out chart. Having allowed 350 g (12 oz) of dressed, trussed and oven-ready turkey per person, decide whether you want a slowly cooked bird or to take it faster.

When stuffing the bird, remember that putting th stuffing in the neck end moistens the breast and add flavour. A body stuffing takes more cooking, an nothing is worse than spooning out soggy, partiall cooked stuffing which nobody really fancies. Nec stuffing also improves the look of the turkey and it i easier to carve.

To test if a turkey is cooked, pierce the thigh with skewer: the juices that run out should be clear.

A stuffing for turkey

Metric

100 g minced veal
Turkey liver, minced
75 g bacon, rind removed, minced
Grated rind of 1 orange
2 × 15 ml spoons chopped fresh parsley
1 × 500 g can unsweetened chestnut purée
1 egg, beaten
Salt
Pepper

Imperial

4 oz minced veal
Turkey liver, minced
3 oz bacon, rind removed, minced
Grated rind of 1 orange
2 tablespoons chopped fresh parsley
1 × 1 lb can unsweetened chestnut purée
1 egg, beaten
Salt
Pepper

Mix all the ingredients thoroughly together with salt and pepper to taste. Stuff the neck of the turkey, working the stuffing well under the skin. Fold the flap under the bird and secure it by sewing or with a skewer. It is important that the stuffing does not come out during cooking.
Makes enough for a 4.5 kg (10 lb) turkey

	Slow Roasting at 160°C, 325°F, Gas Mark 3	Quick Roasting, loosely wrapped in foil, at 230°C, 450°F, Gas Mark 8
2.75–3.5kg (6–8 lb)	3–3½ hours	2¼–2½ hours
3.5–4.5 kg (8–10 lb)	3½–3¾ hours	2½–2¾ hours
4.5–6 kg (10–14 lb)	3¾–4½ hours	2¾–3 hours
6–8 kg (14–18 lb)	4¼–4¾ hours	3–3½ hours

Right: Boiled turkey;
Far right: Roast turkey
and gammon

Boiled turkey

Metric	Imperial
1 turkey	*1 turkey*
1 head of celery, chopped	*1 head of celery, chopped*
500 g carrots, peeled and chopped	*1 lb carrots, peeled and chopped*
6 onions, peeled and quartered	*6 onions, peeled and quartered*
2 garlic cloves	*2 garlic cloves*
225 g piece collar bacon	*8 oz piece collar bacon*
2 pigs' feet, split	*2 pigs' feet, split*
3 bay leaves	*3 bay leaves*
Salt	*Salt*
Pepper	*Pepper*
Parsley sprigs to garnish	*Parsley sprigs to garnish*

Cooking Time: 12 minutes per 500 g (1 lb)

This is one of the most successful ways to cook a turkey as it finishes moist and full of flavour, and there is enough stock left for a soup. For buffet parties, the stock may be reduced by boiling and then chilled until set and jellied. This jellied stock, chopped, makes an attractive garnish for the sliced meat.

Put all the ingredients with salt and pepper to taste into a big ham kettle and cover with water. Bring to the boil and skim. Simmer for 12 minutes per 500 g (1 lb). Remove from the heat and allow the turkey to cool in the pan. Serve the cold turkey sliced, garnished with the chopped jellied stock, if liked, and parsley sprigs.

Roast turkey and gammon

Metric	Imperial
1 × 4.5 kg turkey (or whatever size you wish)	*1 × 10 lb turkey (or whatever size you wish)*
1 × 1.5–2 kg piece of gammon bacon (size to fit the bird's cavity), soaked in cold water overnight	*1 × 3–4 lb piece of gammon bacon (size to fit the bird's cavity), soaked in cold water overnight*
2 bay leaves	*2 bay leaves*
50 g butter, softened	*2 oz butter, softened*
Salt	*Salt*
Pepper	*Pepper*
Watercress to garnish	*Watercress to garnish*

Cooking Time: 4–4¾ hours
Oven: 160°C, 325°F, Gas Mark 3

This is a lot of trouble, but is well repaid by the result.
With a sharp knife separate the rib cage from the flesh of the turkey and, with poultry shears, cut out the rib cage. Cut the bacon roughly to fit inside the bird. Put the bacon in a pan with the bay leaves, cover with cold water and bring to the boil. Cover and simmer for 45 minutes. Remove and allow to cool.
Strip off the rind and fat and put the bacon in the turkey, making the best shape you can. Place in a roasting tin. Spread the softened butter over the turkey, sprinkle with salt and pepper and cover with foil. Roast in a preheated moderate oven for 3½ to 3¾ hours.
If it is difficult to carve the turkey and the bacon at the same time, remove the bacon and slice it separately. Serve garnished with watercress.
Serves 12

Turkey escalopes viennoise

Metric	Imperial
4 × 150 g turkey steaks	4 × 5 oz turkey steaks
1 egg	1 egg
Salt	Salt
Pepper	Pepper
40–50 g dry breadcrumbs	1½–2 oz dry breadcrumbs
50 g butter	2 oz butter
2 × 15 ml spoons oil	2 tablespoons oil
To garnish:	To garnish:
12 anchovy fillets	12 anchovy fillets
1 hard-boiled egg	1 hard-boiled egg
1 × 5 ml spoon capers	1 teaspoon capers

Cooking Time: 10 minutes

Commercial turkey steaks are cut by machine from raw turkey breasts. A very sharp knife and considerable skill would be required to produce them at home. They are very good, and treated correctly make an excellent substitute for veal in this classic dish.

Put the steaks on a board and beat them as flat and thin as you can. Beat the egg with salt and pepper. Dip the steaks in the egg, then coat in the breadcrumbs.

Melt the butter with the oil in a frying pan and fry the steaks for 5 minutes on each side. Transfer the escalopes to a warmed serving platter. Garnish with a trellis of anchovy fillets, sieved hard-boiled egg (the white separated from the yolk) and capers.

Turkey and gammon pie

Metric	Imperial
50 g butter	2 oz butter
2 onions, peeled and minced	2 onions, peeled and minced
2 garlic cloves, crushed	2 garlic cloves, crushed
500 g turkey meat, finely diced	1 lb turkey meat, finely diced
225 g gammon, finely diced	8 oz gammon, finely diced
40 g plain flour	1½ oz plain flour
600 ml turkey or chicken stock	1 pint turkey or chicken stock
Salt	Salt
Pepper	Pepper
225 g mushrooms, sliced	8 oz mushrooms, sliced
225 g frozen puff pastry, thawed	8 oz frozen puff pastry, thawed
1 egg, beaten	1 egg, beaten

Cooking Time: 1½ hours
Oven: 200°C, 400°F, Gas Mark 6
    180°C, 350°F, Gas Mark 4

Melt the butter in a saucepan and fry the onions and garlic until soft but not brown. Add the turkey and gammon. Sprinkle with the flour and cook, stirring, for 1 minute. Stir in the stock. Season with salt and pepper to taste. Remove from the heat and add the mushrooms. Turn into a 1.2 l (2 pint) capacity pie dish and allow to cool.

Cover the dish with puff pastry, make an airhole and decorate with the pastry trimmings. Brush with beaten egg and bake in a preheated moderately hot oven for 45 minutes. Reduce the heat to moderate and bake for a further 30 minutes. If the pastry gets too brown, cover with damp greaseproof paper.

Turkey escalopes viennoise;
Turkey and gammon pie

Turkey croquettes

Metric	Imperial
500 g cooked turkey meat, minced	1 lb cooked turkey meat, minced
1 onion, peeled and minced	1 onion, peeled and minced
1 × 5 ml spoon dried tarragon	1 teaspoon dried tarragon
15 g butter, melted	½ oz butter, melted
75 g cooked ham, minced	3 oz cooked ham, minced
Salt	Salt
Pepper	Pepper
2 eggs, beaten	2 eggs, beaten
40–50 g dry breadcrumbs	1½–2 oz dry breadcrumbs
Oil for deep frying	Oil for deep frying

Cooking Time: 7–8 minutes

Mix together the turkey, onion, tarragon, melted butter, ham, salt and pepper to taste and one of the eggs. Shape into 8 croquettes. Dip in the remaining beaten egg, then coat with the breadcrumbs.

Deep fry in oil heated to 185°C, 360°F for 7 to 8 minutes or until golden brown. Drain on absorbent kitchen paper and serve hot.

Makes 8

Fricassée of turkey

Metric	Imperial
50 g butter	2 oz butter
1 onion, peeled and finely chopped	1 onion, peeled and finely chopped
750 g turkey pieces	1½ lb turkey pieces
40 g plain flour	1½ oz plain flour
600 ml turkey or chicken stock	1 pint turkey or chicken stock
225 g mushrooms, sliced	8 oz mushrooms, sliced
1 × 5 ml spoon dried tarragon	1 teaspoon dried tarragon
Salt	Salt
Pepper	Pepper
150 ml double cream	¼ pint double cream
Chopped parsley to garnish	Chopped parsley to garnish

Cooking Time: About 1¾ hours

Melt the butter in a saucepan. Add the onion and turkey pieces and fry until the turkey pieces are lightly browned. Sprinkle the flour into the pan and cook, stirring, for 1 minute. Stir in the stock and stir until it thickens. Add the mushrooms, tarragon and salt and pepper to taste. Cover and simmer very gently, stirring from time to time, for 1½ hours.

Transfer the turkey pieces to a warmed serving dish. Keep hot. Stir the cream into the casserole, adjust the seasoning and pour over the turkey. Sprinkle with chopped parsley and serve.

Curried turkey

Metric	Imperial
50 g butter	2 oz butter
2 × 15 ml spoons hot curry powder	2 tablespoons hot curry powder
2 onions, peeled and chopped	2 onions, peeled and chopped
2 garlic cloves, crushed	2 garlic cloves, crushed
750 g cooked turkey meat, finely diced	1½ lb cooked turkey meat, finely diced
600 ml turkey or chicken stock	1 pint turkey or chicken stock
1 × 15 ml spoon tomato purée	1 tablespoon tomato purée
1 × 15 ml spoon sugar	1 tablespoon sugar
Juice of 1 lemon	Juice of 1 lemon
Salt	Salt
Pepper	Pepper
2 bay leaves	2 bay leaves
1 fresh thyme sprig	1 fresh thyme sprig

Cooking Time: About 1¼ hours

Melt the butter in a saucepan. Add the curry powder, onions and garlic and fry until softened. Add the turkey and stir in the stock, tomato purée, sugar, lemon juice, salt and pepper to taste and the herbs. Cover and simmer for 1 hour.

If the curry is not hot enough, fry some more curry powder in butter in a separate pan and add it to the turkey mixture. Remove the bay leaf before serving, with curry accompaniments.

Turkey croquettes

Fricassée of turkey

Curried turkey

Left: Turkey pâté de campagne
Below: Turkey breast in aspic

Cold turkey dishes

Turkey pâté de campagne

Metric	Imperial
225 g butter, melted	8 oz butter, melted
2 onions, peeled and minced	2 onions, peeled and minced
2 garlic cloves, crushed	2 garlic cloves, crushed
750 g turkey meat, minced	1½ lb turkey meat, minced
225 g fat smoked bacon, rind removed, minced	8 oz fat smoked bacon, rind removed, minced
1 turkey liver, minced	1 turkey liver, minced
225 g chicken livers, minced	8 oz chicken livers, minced
1 × 15 ml spoon tomato purée	1 tablespoon tomato purée
150 ml dry red wine	¼ pint dry red wine
1 × 15 ml spoon dried tarragon	1 tablespoon dried tarragon
150 ml turkey or chicken stock	¼ pint turkey or chicken stock
Salt	Salt
Pepper	Pepper
2 bay leaves	2 bay leaves

Cooking Time: About 2¾ hours
Oven: 180°C, 350°F, Gas Mark 4

Heat 25 g (1 oz) of the butter in a frying pan. Add the onions and garlic and fry until softened. Mix together the remaining ingredients, except the bay leaves, with salt and pepper to taste and add the onions, garlic and remaining butter. Turn into a terrine. Put the bay leaves on top, cover and bake in a preheated moderate oven for 2½ hours. Cool under a weighted plate.

Serves 8 to 10

Turkey breast in aspic

Metric	Imperial
500–750 g cooked turkey breast, skinned and sliced	1–1½ lb cooked turkey breast, skinned and sliced
1½ × 70 g packets aspic jelly powder	1½ × 2½ oz packets aspic jelly powder
900 ml turkey or chicken stock	1½ pints turkey or chicken stock
Fresh tarragon sprigs, blanched and refreshed in cold water to garnish	Fresh tarragon sprigs, blanched and refreshed in cold water to garnish

Arrange the sliced turkey on a shallow dish. Make up the aspic with the stock, according to the directions on the packet. Allow to cool until on the point of setting. Pour most of the aspic over the turkey and the remainder into a separate dish. Chill until set.

Chop the extra aspic finely and use to garnish the turkey aspic with the sprigs of tarragon.

Index

PDO 81-140